# THE GREAT BRITISH
# ROAD RIDES GUIDE

## CLIVE FORTH

B L O O M S B U R Y

LONDON · NEW DELHI · NEW YORK · SYDNEY

**Note**

While every effort has been made to ensure that the content of this book is as technically accurate and as sound as possible, neither the author nor the publishers can accept responsibility for
any injury or loss sustained as a result of the use of this material.

Published by Bloomsbury Publishing Plc
50 Bedford Square
London WC1B 3DP
www.bloomsbury.com
Bloomsbury is a trademark of Bloomsbury Publishing Plc

First edition 2013

Copyright © 2014 Clive Forth

ISBN (print): 978-1-4081-7943-7
ISBN (ePdf): 978-1-4729-1146-9
ISBN (EPUB): 978-1-4729-1159-9

A CIP catalogue record for this book is available from the British Library.

**Acknowledgements**

Cover photograph and inside photographs © Frazer Waller, with the exception of pages: 53 and 110 © Shutterstock; 97 (top), 98 and 112 © Tim Ireland/PA Wire/PA Images; 97 (bottom) and 109 © Pete Goding/GodingImages/PA Images; 100 © David Davies/PA Wire/PA Images; and 101 © Thomas van Bracht/Demotix/Demotix/PA Images.
Each of the route maps contains Ordnance Survey data © Crown copyright 2014 Ordnance Survey 100055/07.
The routes and the elevation profiles were created using Clive's Garmin GPS device.

This book is produced using paper that is made from wood grown in managed, sustainable forests. It is natural, renewable and recyclable. The logging and manufacturing processes conform to the environmental regulations of the country of origin.

Typeset in 9.5pt on 13pt Myriad Pro by Margaret Brain, Wisbech, Cambs

Printed and bound in China by Leo Paper Products

10 9 8 7 6 5 4 3 2 1

# CONTENTS

# INTRODUCTION

Like many of you I've ridden bicycles for pretty much my entire life. As a child I used to sit and watch The Milk Race and Tour de France before heading off on my mini 'racer' around the lanes where I grew up. I'd spend hours and hours planning routes on an Ordnance Survey map, trying to link fun-flowing sections of road to those 'massive' hills in an attempt to replicate those iconic Alpine climbs. All I ever wanted to do was ride bikes for a living, I loved it that much (and still do).

By a twist of fate my beloved road bike was stolen and I ended up with a mountain bike as a replacement. My cycling career flourished as I grew through my teens but it was mountain biking that paved the way for that career on two wheels.

My father encouraged me to join the local cycling club and I would head out with them in the winter months on the trails. In the summer the old guys would get their road bikes out and I'd join them on the regular weekend runs. Suffice to say this was hard work on knobby tyres, it did however get me very fit.

My mountain bike career flourished and I left school to race for some prestigious teams. Road bicycles were always there as training aids but at the time they played second fiddle to the mountain bike. But as many of my close friends continued to race on the road, and most of them became very accomplished, inevitably their enthusiasm rubbed off on me.

A few years ago a truly magical thing happened when I met the love of my life Daria. A chance meeting in a local cycle shop cafe turned into three days of riding bikes and, well, the rest is history. Now the reason this had such a profound effect on me was not only had I found the love of my life and my soulmate but this incredible woman had rekindled my spirit for the love of all things cycling.

Daria is from Tuscany and a very accomplished racer both on road and off – she is an amazing athlete and inspiration. Just before we got married she'd taken a job in the French Alps, the road bike was pulled out of the shed and before I knew it I was chasing her up Alpine climbs, living out my childhood dreams.

My cycling career has taken me all over the British Isles on many adventures. Throughout my journeys I've ridden and seen some absolutely stunning scenery and sections of road. Having just completed my previous book title *The Great British Mountain Bike Trail Guide* it just made sense to continue the road trip taking in the best of British, only this time on the road. The guys at Boardman Bikes kindly furnished me with the latest elite SLR model while sponsors Mavic and Garmin finished the package, enabling me to navigate my way around with speed and grace on some of Britain's finest asphalt.

**Clive Forth**

# How to use this book

With Daria's assistance (she's ridden all over the world using various guidebooks) we set out the basic concept of the book. It needed to incorporate some shorter training rides within easy reach of major conurbations and some longer more challenging rides taking in tough climbs, fun descents and superb scenery.

For the start point I wanted somewhere that was easily accessible and easy to locate. We have a fantastic rail network to accompany the plethora of roads in the UK and it made sense to use this network to access the rides.

The rides start from railway stations on the main network (with a few exceptions). It's easy to use the national rail network to get you to the start of each ride from anywhere in the country, and you will find easy parking, accommodation and all the usual amenities nearby a railway station making for an obvious start point. Information including coordinates and postcode is located at the start of each ride.

The maps provided will give you an overview of the general area and the route descriptions have been kept relatively brief. I have done my best to avoid busy roads and complicated junctions but inevitably there is the odd occasion where you simply can't avoid such things.

As opposed to ruining your purchase by tearing out route cards, or bending the spine in an attempt to photocopy from the book, we have created route cards that you can download from the Bloomsbury website at: www.bloomsbury. com/9781408179437. You can also download GPX files for each route from the Garmin Connect website.

At the start of each route you'll find information on key climbs and total elevation gain. I have indicated the overall distance and a route profile, which will give you an idea of the severity of the ride – this will enable you to calculate how long you need to allow to ride each route. With such a wide variety in people's capabilities I did not want to add an estimated time as this is something you can easily calculate yourself.

## GETTING YOUR BIKE ON A TRAIN

If you choose to take advantage of the fantastic rail network to get around then do check with the service provider in advance regarding the specific rules on taking bicycles. Each train company will have slightly different guidelines and bicycles may need to be booked on in advance. At peak times it may not be possible to take your bike on busy commuter routes. You can find lots of useful information on the National Rail website.

www.nationalrail.co.uk/stations_destinations/cyclists.aspx

www.nationalrail.co.uk/tocs_maps/tocs/TrainOperators.aspx

## CHECKLIST

Before you set out it goes without saying that you should make sure your bike is in good working order and fit for the job. This checklist may help.

- Check the brakes work and you have sufficient life in the brake blocks, also make sure they contact the rim and do not rub the tyre or drop towards the spokes

- Check the brake and gear cables are in good condition

- The wheels should be inserted and tightened according to the manufacturers' guidelines

- Make sure your wheels spin free and are true, check for loose spokes and adjust accordingly

- Your tyres must be in good condition and inflated to the manufacturers' recommended pressure

- The chain and drive system must be in good working order, sufficiently lubricated but not bathing in oil

- The saddle must be in good condition and adjusted to the correct height and angle

- Bar tapes/grips and hoods must be in good condition

- You should also carry sufficient spares including:
    - ☐ Inner tube
    - ☐ Patch kit (you may want to include a tyre patch)
    - ☐ Tyre levers
    - ☐ Pump
    - ☐ Chain tool/multi tool and specific tools for your bike (chain quick links are a handy addition)
    - ☐ Navigation aids, route card, OS map, GPS device
    - ☐ Mobile phone, charged and switched off
    - ☐ Money, cash and cards
    - ☐ Spare clothing, windproof, waterproof (tailor your clothing to suit the conditions).

## EXPOSURE

The exposure grade before each route will give you an idea of the type of terrain that surrounds you and how likely you are to encounter strong winds and inclement weather (particularly in spring, autumn and winter). A ride with a high exposure rating should be approached with caution in poor weather, and you should pack additional clothing.

Some of the rides will take you out into remote areas, keep an eye on weather forecasts and let someone know where you are going and when you anticipate returning. Always respect the rules of the road and wear some bright clothes. And above all enjoy yourself.

## Route Analysis

Total number of routes: 55
Total distance for all routes: 4470.2 km
Total metres climbed on all routes: 67,471m

### Routes under 50km: 9

1   Oxenhope: Taste Le Tour, part 4 30km
2   Longniddry: Golfers Galore 34km
3   Linlithgow: Beecraigs Blast 35.5km
4   Brighton and Hove 1: Ditchling Dilemma 37km
5   Tring 2: A Playboy's Playground 40km
6   Keswick: Buttermere Blast 45km
7   Brighton and Hove 2: Peacehaven Pedal 48km
8   Southampton, New Forest 1: Bolderwood Bowl 48km
9   Banbury 2: Two-Stroke Blues 48km

### Routes 50km to 80km: 25

10  Exeter 3: A Trip to the Sea 50km
11  Southampton, New Forest 2: Brockenhurst Bash 52km
12  Tring 1: Chiltern Classics 53.8km
13  Barnstaple 2: Ilfracombe Rollers 54km
14  Milngavie: Jamie's Jewel 54km
15  Wendover 1: Great Missenden Mission 54km
16  Oxenhope: Taste Le Tour, part 3 56.5km
17  Beauly: We Are Glass 63km
18  Hereford 2: Literary Loop 64km
19  Settle 1: Littondale Loop 64km
20  Hexham 2: Hartside Haul 68km

21  Sanquhar: Leadhills Leg Burner 68km
22  Church Stretton 2: The Short Sting 68.4km
23  Dumfries: Dalbeattie Dash 68.5km
24  Leyburn: Taste Le Tour, part 2 70km
25  Moffat: Moffat Mash-Up 70.5km
26  Betws-y-Coed 2: Take it to the Slate 72km
27  Dunblane: Dance of the Naughty Knight 72km
28  Lockerbie 2: Tibetan Twist 72km
29  Fort William: Moy Ahoy 73.5km
30  Buxton: Trip for a Tart 74km
31  Exmoor: Minehead Mash-Up 74km
32  Wendover 2: Ludgershall Loop 75km
33  Exeter 2: Point to Point 78km
34  Inverness: In Search of the Monster 78.5km

### Routes 80km to 100km: 7

35  Banbury 1: Shakespeare's World 82km
36  Betws-y-Coed 1: The Snowdon Sneaky Lap 82km
37  Windermere 1: The 30% 84km
38  Llandovery: Search for the Stig 86km
39  Barnstaple 1: Exford Expedition 88km
40  Hexham 1: Stanhope Stoker 88km
41  Penrith 1: Brampton Bash 98km

### Routes over 100km: 14

42  Applecross: A Coastal Cruise 102km
43  Achnasheen: The Torridon Terror 103km
44  Church Stretton 1: The Sting 104km
45  Exeter 1, Dartmoor: Furry Hands 104km
46  Windermere 2: Tebay Tester 104km
47  Settle 2: Dale Delight 110km
48  Leyburn: Taste Le Tour, part 1 113km
49  Lockerbie 1: Moffat Mission 115km
50  Glenfinnan: West Coast Wonder 130km

51  Hereford 1: Black Mountain Blast
    146km
52  Tarbet: The Rest & Be Thankful 152km
53  Penrith 2: The Penrith Pennine Punisher
    154km
54  Leeds: Tour de France: Le Tour 2014
    Grand Depart (Stage 1) 206km
55  York: Tour de France: Le Tour 2014
    (Stage 2) 208km

*Three longest routes excluding Le Tour 2014:*

■  Penrith 2: The Penrith Pennine Punisher
   154km
■  Tarbet: The Rest & Be Thankful 152km
■  Glenfinnan: West Coast Wonder 130km

*Shortest route:*

■  Oxenhope: Taste Le Tour, part 4 30km

*Three routes with the most climbing (excluding Le Tour 2014):*

■  Penrith 2: The Penrith Pennine Punisher
   2559m
■  Tarbet: The Rest & Be Thankful 2448m
■  Exeter 1, Dartmoor: Furry Hands 2186m

*Route with the least climbing:*

■  Longniddry: Golfers Galore 196m

*Routes that climb:*

*Under 500m: 3*

■  Longniddry: Golfers Galore 196m
■  Southampton, New Forest 1:
   Bolderwood Bowl 272m
■  Southampton, New Forest 2:
   Brockenhurst Bash 365m

*500m–1000m: 19*

■  Brighton and Hove 1: Ditchling
   Dilemma 510m

■  Tring 2: A Playboy's Playground 512m
■  Banbury 2: Two-Stroke Blues 517m
■  Hereford 2: Literary Loop 542m
■  Linlithgow: Beecraigs Blast 590m
■  Exeter 3: A Trip to the Sea 600m
■  Dumfries: Dalbeattie Dash 670m
■  Brighton and Hove 2: Peacehaven Pedal
   688m
■  Wendover 2: Ludgershall Loop 700m
■  Tring 1: Chiltern Classics 717m
■  Banbury 1: Shakespeare's World 750m
■  Milngavie: Jamie's Jewel 757m
■  Oxenhope: Taste Le Tour, part 4 763m
■  Inverness: In Search of the Monster
   790m
■  Beauly: We Are Glass 832m
■  Dunblane: Dance of the Naughty Knight
   895m
■  Wendover 1: Great Missenden Mission
   914m
■  Fort William: Moy Ahoy 922m
■  Sanquhar: Leadhills Leg Burner 952m

*1001m–1500m: 17*

■  Keswick: Buttermere Blast 1017m
■  Leyburn: Taste Le Tour, part 2 1026m
■  Lockerbie 2: Tibetan Twist 1040m
■  Settle 1: Littondale Loop 1063m
■  Church Stretton 2: The Short Sting
   1069m
■  Barnstaple 2: Ilfracombe Rollers 1125m
■  Hexham 2: Hartside Haul 1146m
■  Moffat: Moffat Mash-Up 1180m
■  Llandovery: Search for the Stig 1213m
■  Penrith 1: Brampton Bash 1217m
■  Oxenhope: Taste Le Tour, part 3 1258m
■  Buxton: Trip for a Tart 1273m
■  Lockerbie 1: Moffat Mission 1352m
■  Betws-y-Coed 1: The Snowdon Sneaky
   Lap 1377m
■  Hexham 1: Stanhope Stonker 1402km

- Achnasheen: The Torridon Terror 1430m
- Betws-y-Coed 2: Take it to the Slate 1488m

*1501m–2000m: 9*

- Settle 2: Dale Delight 1524m
- Exmoor: Minehead Mash-Up 1544m
- Windermere 2: Tebay Tester 1568m
- Church Stretton 1: The Sting 1572m
- Exeter 2: Point to Point 1582m
- Barnstaple 1: Exford Expedition 1585m
- Leyburn: Taste Le Tour, part 1 1685m
- Hereford 1: Black Mountain Blast 1733m

- Windermere 1: The 30% 1927m

*Over 2000m: 7*

- Applecross: A Coastal Cruise 2054m
- Exeter 1 Dartmoor: Furry Hands 2186m
- Glenfinnan: West Coast Wonder 2186m
- Tarbet: The Rest & Be Thankful 2448m
- Penrith 2: The Penrith Pennine Punisher 2559m
- Leeds: Tour de France: Le Tour 2014 Grand Depart (Stage 1) 2595m
- York: Tour de France: Le Tour 2014 (Stage 2) 3633m

## RIDE STYLES EXPLAINED

If the route is not a loop there are two options:

**Point to point** – These rides have a different end point to the start point, the rides have been created so you can use the rail network to get back to your start point. These rides can also be turned into much longer 'out and back' rides should you wish to do so.

**Out and back** – This type of ride will involve riding the same sections of road in both directions, from your start point a route will take you to a point of interest, here you can refuel or do an overnight stop before making your return journey.

# THE
# SOUTH-WEST

# BARNSTAPLE 1: EXFORD EXPEDITION

**Start point:** Barnstaple railway station

**Grid ref:** SS 55593 32552

**Postcode:** EX31 2AU

**Total distance:** 88km

**Total elevation:** 1585m

**Max elevation:** 422m

## KEY CLIMBS

**From km 0 to km 12.5:** 236m climb over 12.5km

**From km 17 to km 21:** 140m climb over 4km

**From km 26.8 to km 29.5:** 148m climb over 2.7km

**From km 44 to km 46.6:** 124m climb over 2.6km

**From km 50 to km 53:** 154m climb over 3km

**Other key elevation gain:** From km 0 to km 57.6: elevation gain of 416m

**Exposure:** 4/5

Barnstaple, which lies to the west of Exmoor on the North Devonshire coast, is your starting point for a classic ride that will take you high up on the moor to the village of Exford. With over 1500m of climbing this is not a ride for the faint-hearted, nor is it a ride for a wet or a windy day. Watch the weather closely as this coastal region is known for fast-changing weather patterns as swells blow in from the Atlantic.

Throughout the ride you will discover some quaint villages and fantastic sections of road with spectacular views over open moorland and the surrounding area, and there are many places to stop off along the way to refuel and take in the beauty of Exmoor National Park.

From the station cross over the River Taw. Taking a left turn at the second round-about, you should pick up signs for the A39 to Ilfracombe. Follow the A road north, climbing up out of town past the North Devon District hospital. The road climbs up into open ground away from the town.

Beyond Shirwell Cross continue following the A39. The road will narrow and descend down through Woolley Wood. Take care on the descent as there is a tight right-hand switchback followed by a

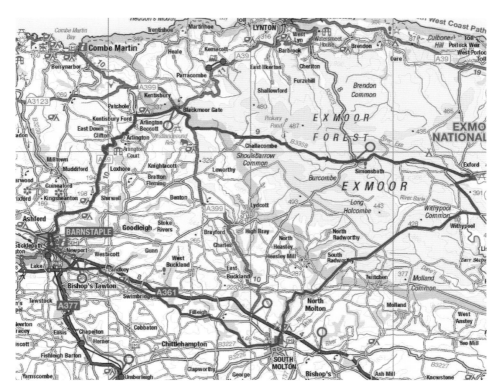

left-hand switchback and a series of tight turns as you drop down towards Arlington Court.

The road continues in a similar vein towards Kentisbury Ford. During the holiday season the roads in this area can become quite busy, so take extra care on the narrower sections where visibility for motorists is hindered by the high hedges and banks.

In the village of Blackmoor Gate take a right turn on to the A399. After just over a kilometre the route forks left on to the B3358 and starts to head uphill towards Challacombe village. You will pass through the village and follow the winding road through the lush green scenery towards Simonsbath. The high hedges do obscure the view but on occasion you get a glimpse of the rolling hillsides as you

head closer to the moor and the village of Exford.

In the village the route takes a right turn just before the stone bridge. If you need to take on board fuel this is an ideal place to do it. The road out of the village

*High hedges line many of the roads in the area.*

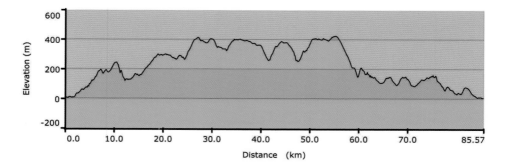

climbs up a steep gradient and takes you up on to the moor. Following the B3223 for a couple of kilometres until you come to a crossroads at Comer's Gate. Here you need to take a right turn and descend down into the village of Withypool, another picturesque village typical of the region.

Just beyond the river the route takes a right turn and climbs up on to open ground to Withypool Common. This lovely climb has a good surface and the gradient is fair. As you crest the hill, passing through open ground, you start to descend slightly. Take care throughout this section as you will cross a cattle grid before a small rise leads you into a long descent.

The descent drops you down into the village of North Molton. High hedges obscure the view but once again you get the odd glimpse of the wonderful rolling

*Withypool village, your last chance to take on supplies before heading up on to the moor.*

*The long but steady climb with stunning views.*

hillsides all around. In the village you cross over the River Mole and climb up out into a wooded section that leads you down to the major A361 trunk road.

Take care while crossing the busy trunk road and continue to head in a southerly direction into South Molton, at the T-junction take a right and pass through the village centre. Following the road markings for Barnstaple before picking up a left turn on to the B3227 heading in a westerly direction signed Torrington.

You will pass over a couple of roundabouts and within a kilometre bear right on to a minor road towards Stags Head, the road sign here is marked Kingsland cross but there is no fingerboard pointing to the right, the fork is preceded by an entrance road on your right-hand side to some industrial looking buildings.

The narrow road twists and turns its way running parallel to the major trunk road and a sweet little descent drops you into the village of Swimbridge. Just a few more kilometres to go and you're back into Barnstaple. Follow the road into the town centre. Complete the loop by picking up where you headed out at the river crossing.

# 2 BARNSTAPLE 2: ILFRACOMBE ROLLERS

**Start point:** Barnstaple railway station

**Grid ref:** SS 55593 32552

**Postcode:** EX31 2AU

**Total distance:** 54km

**Total elevation:** 1125m

**Max elevation:** 305m

## KEY CLIMBS

**From km 0 to km 14:** 245m climb over 14km

**From km 26 to km 33:** 295m climb over 7km

**From km 41 to km 43:** 118m climb over 2km

**Other key elevation gain:** From km 0 to km 20.9: elevation gain of 302m

**Exposure:** 3/5

*The road hugs the north Devonshire Coast, dropping through Combe Martin.*

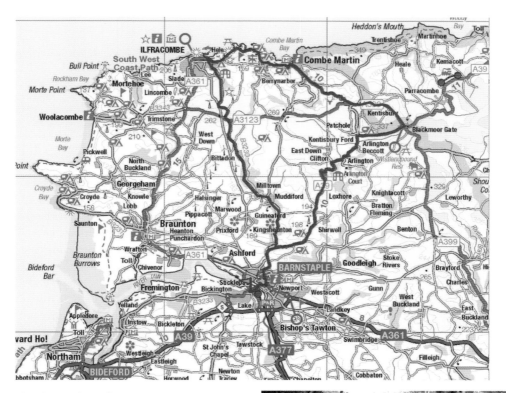

The shorter loop from Barnstaple will take you northwards to the coast and the town of Ilfracombe. Here you traverse along next to the sea through a series of sizable rolling hills before dropping into the seaside village of Combe Martin. From here you head back inland in a southerly direction through some spectacular scenery and twisty roads towards your start point of Barnstaple railway station.

From the station bear right at the roundabout crossing over the river, the road bears round to the right and at the second roundabout take a left turn on to the A39 heading towards Ilfracombe, the steep gradients lead you up out of town past the hospital, in just under a kilometre you bear left on to the B3230, the road winds its way along through woodland next to Bradiford Water.

*Fast-rolling asphalt lead to stunning coastal views.*

After a couple of kilometres you will pass through the village of Muddiford and Milltown, the surface throughout this section is great and there is lots of interest to the road as it twists and winds its way along heading towards the sea.

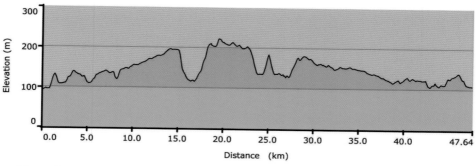

A long descent drops you down into Ilfracombe. If you wish to visit the town take a left at the junction with traffic lights for the town centre. But if you wish to continue on the route take a right turn, switching back on to the A399 and dropping downhill. This section of road is very popular with tourists as it links the major towns on the North Devonshire coast. Throughout this section of road you will descend and ascend some steep gradients. There are some great views of the rocky coastline as you make your way to Combe Martin Bay.

Passing Hele Bay on your left you climb up to a viewpoint. It's worth taking time

*The North Devon coast and its many hidden bays.*

out here to savour the scenery. The road then drops down past Widmouth Head and Watermouth Castle before you swing inland slightly, traversing the cliff tops once more before dropping down into the village of Combe Martin.

You will now head inland along the valley away from the sea. The climb up from Combe Martin is long, but it's a relatively easy one: the gradient is fair and the surface is good. You will come into the village of Blackmoor Gate where you need to take a right turn on to the A39 back towards Barnstaple.

The main road winds its way back through open countryside and as you approach Arlington Court on your left you start to climb up through Woolley Wood and on to Garman's Down. Once again this route is popular with tourists so care should be taken on the sections that narrow down as the high hedges obscure the visibility for motorists and larger traffic may be taking up more than its half of the road.

You will descend back into Barnstaple on the same road that you took on your outbound route, simply retrace your steps through the town centre back to the railway station where you started the ride. The town is packed with many restaurants, cafes and bars where you can refuel for your next adventure.

# 3  EXETER 1, DARTMOOR: FURRY HANDS

**Start point:** Exeter St Davids railway station

**Grid ref:** SX 91248 93310

**Postcode:** EX4 4NT

**Total distance:** 104km

**Total elevation:** 2186m

**Max elevation:** 450m

## KEY CLIMBS

**From km 0 to km 7.6:** 166m climb over 7.6km

**From km 13.3 to km 19.3:** 232m climb over 6km

**From km 21.8 to km 31.2:** 264m climb over 9.6km

**From km 48.5 to km 50:** 120m climb over 1.5km

**From km 56.8 to km 69.8:** 326m climb over 13km

**From km 81.2 to km 92.2:** 204m climb over 11km

**Other key elevation gain:** From km 0 to km 31.2: elevation gain of 434m

**Exposure:** 5/5

Dartmoor is known for its rugged scenery, rocky outcrops and mires. This ride will take you higher up on to the moor heading out towards Princetown home of the famous Dartmoor Prison, before heading southwards and back in an easterly direction towards the start point in Exeter.

The moor itself covers in the region of a thousand square kilometres and is alleged to be the largest granite area within the British Isles. You will have some spectacular views as you ride on to some of the highest points on the moor passing the many tors (hilltops) along the way. It should be noted that the moor can be very unforgiving, with weather systems changing rapidly. The area is known for high winds and rain, so watch the weather and choose the day to ride wisely. Make sure you take ample warm and waterproof clothing if there is the slightest hint of precipitation.

From the railway station take a right turn on the A377 Bonhay Road heading south. You will have the river to your right-hand side as you do so. In just over a kilometre you will reach a major

*Quiet lanes and stiff climbs as you head out into the National Park.*

Just beyond St Thomas station you pass through the district of St Thomas, climbing uphill slightly while heading to the outskirts of town. The climb steepens as you crest the hill before dropping down another steep gradient and passing underneath a major trunk road, beyond which is a short sharp steep climb.

The opening kilometres are predominantly climbing. You do get some relief with flatter sections and downhills as you pass through the villages of Longdown and Dunsford. Having passed over the River Teign in Dunsford the road climbs up through the treeline. This is a very picturesque part of the ride and you are nicely sheltered as the road hugs the hillside.

The next leg takes you up to Moretonhampstead. Just before the village the road dips down steeply through some tight corners before climbing up through a tight switchback into the village. You will need to crossover the A382 in the centre of the village. Take care here as the visibility is poor.

You will now be well on your way to Two Bridges, the furthest west that this route will take you. Beyond Moretonhampstead continue to climb up towards the main moor. Up here there is little shelter, and you are really exposed to the elements. This is the section of the ride that gives it the name Furry Hand. It is reported that two separate individuals from the Royal Marines have reported strange sightings resulting in an accident while driving this road on a typically foggy Dartmoor night. The legend has it that a pair of severed hairy hands appear on your steering wheel or handlebars and violently steer your vehicle off the road.

intersection, a large roundabout circling above the river. Here you need to take the fourth exit to the right joining the B3212 to Moretonhampstead. Almost immediately after the intersection you will drop underneath the railway line. This is a good indicator that you're on the right route.

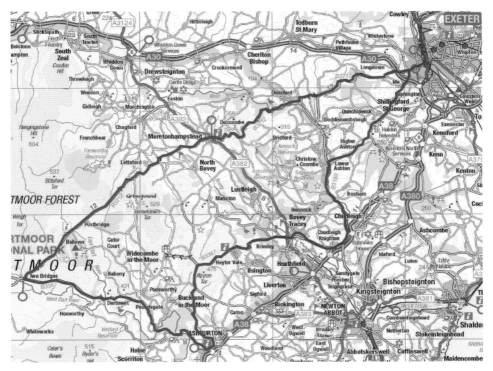

You will descend down into the small village of Postbridge. Here you pass over the East Dart River where the famous Clapper Bridge still remains, which you can see to your left as you pass over the river. Just beyond the village you will drop down to a junction where you need to take a left turn switching back on to the B3357 signposted towards Dartmeet.

The road then traverses across open ground and when you reach a small woodland you descend down the steep hill with some tight corners into the village of Dartmeet. Take care on the steep gradient as the road is very narrow through the blind corners. Beyond the village you will be presented with a tough climb that lasts for just over a kilometre, bringing you back up high on to the moor at Sherberton Common.

The road continues in a similar vein, winding its way across open hillside as you head in a south-easterly direction towards Ashburton. By this point the B road would have finished and become a

*The Clapper Bridge.*

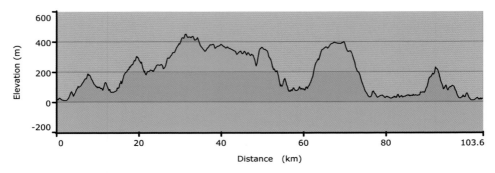

*There are some tough steep climbs on the South side of the National Park.*

minor C road. This changes in the village of Ashburton and the minor C road becomes a B road once again (the B3352). Follow this road through into the centre of the village where you take a left turn on to a minor road signposted to Widecombe and Buckland. After a few hundred metres the road then swings left over a small stream signposted towards Widecombe.

This route climbs gently and after approximately two kilometres you come into a wooded section where you need to take a right turn. The finger signpost points you to Widecombe. This minor road will lead you back up on to the moor past Buckland Common and towards Hemsworthy Gate. Up at Hemsworthy Gate the route switchbacks right on to

the B3387. You now enter a lovely section descending through some fantastic flowing corners.

The narrow road leads you back to the main A382 at Bovey Tracey. Here, cross over the A road and continue on the B3344 towards Chudleigh Knighton. Beyond the village you join on to the B3193 running parallel to the river and the main trunk road. Keep left at a fork in the road and follow the B3193 running parallel with the river towards Lower Ashton. Here in Lower Ashton the route takes a right turn over the River Teign. Climbing up towards Higher Ashton, you will find yourself back on minor roads heading towards Exeter, passing Haldon Forest Park on the right-hand side.

The final descent back towards Exeter is fast and rough in parts. Care should be taken as you enter the village of Ide as the road narrows significantly. Beyond the village take a left turn and within a few hundred metres a right turn (just after you've passed under the main trunk road). The road runs back on itself before turning left and climbing up the steep incline to a T-junction, joining your outward-bound route. To complete the route, simply take a right turn and drop down the hill, retracing your steps through the district of St Thomas back to the main railway station.

# 4 EXETER 2: POINT TO POINT

**Start point:** Exeter St Davids railway station

**Grid ref:** SX 91248 99310

**Postcode:** EX4 4NT

**End point:** Ivybridge train station

**Grid ref:** SX 64739 56542

**Postcode:** PL21 0DQ

**Total distance:** 78km

**Total elevation:** 1582m

**Max elevation:** 450m

## KEY CLIMBS

**From km 0 to km 7.6:** 166m climb over 7.6km

**From km 13.3 to km 19.3:** 232m climb over 6km

**From km 21.8 to km 31.2:** 264m climb over 9.6km

**Exposure:** 5/5

This ride takes you from Exeter across to Ivybridge on the far side of the moor. From here you can get the train back into Exeter, alternatively you can retrace your steps back across the moor or navigate your way along the many narrow lanes running parallel to the A38 trunk road. This route will take you up across the moor, passing through Moretonhampsted, Two Bridges, Princetown and on to Yelverton. Here the route swings left and drops southwards, skirting around the edge of the moor to Ivybridge.

*A weathered milestone high on the moor.*

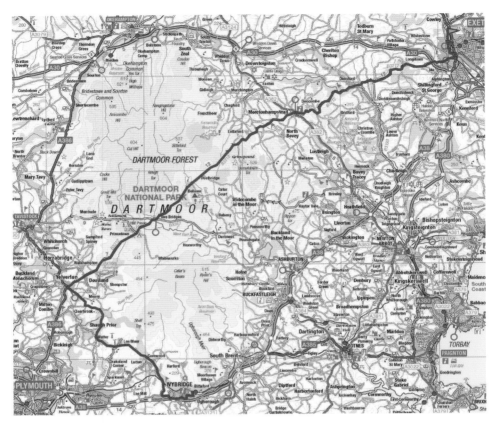

*This remote leg of the ride can be tough on windy and wet days but the views on a sunny clear day are magnificent.*

For details on the opening leg leading you to Two Bridges see pages 9–11. At the T-junction roll downhill round to the right heading towards Princetown on the B3212. The route passes Princetown, home of Her Majesty's Prison Dartmoor. From here you will descend down off the moor, passing the many remains of an ancient settlement. Watch out for the cattle grid as you enter the treeline on a fast straight section!

Down in the village of Yelverton you will come to a roundabout. Pass straight over the roundabout and within a few metres take a road to your left signposted to Meavy and Cadover Bridge. The road then climbs uphill on to Callisham Down. There are some spectacular views up here and

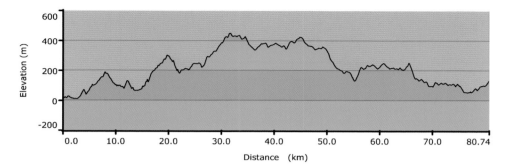

the scenery is a little bit more sympathetic than over on the main moor. The route continues to follow this superb stretch of road towards Cadover Bridge.

You will re-enter the National Park in this next section. Continue to follow the road that you are on, ignoring any turn-offs, as you descend down to the bridge. Be prepared to bear right as you pass over the River Plym. Within a couple of kilometres you arrive at a crossroads where you need to take a left turn signposted to the village of Wotter. Pass through the village and continue to follow the road towards Ivybridge. The road narrows as it climbs up and over a small hill before dropping down underneath the railway. Continue to follow this route down towards the major trunk road. Pick up the signs for the town centre and follow the main route through the town, passing over the river and round to the railway station.

*Little shelter for the elements upon the moor.*

# 5 EXETER 3: A TRIP TO THE SEA

**Start point:** Exeter St Davids railway station

**Grid ref:** SX 91248 93310

**Postcode:** EX4 4NT

**Total distance:** 50km

**Total elevation:** 600m

**Max elevation:** 172m

## KEY CLIMBS

**From km 10 to km 20:** 148m climb over 10 km

**From km 26.2 to km 37.5:** 163m climb over 11.3km

**Exposure:** 1/5

*Mellow gradients and wooded lanes lead you to the coast.*

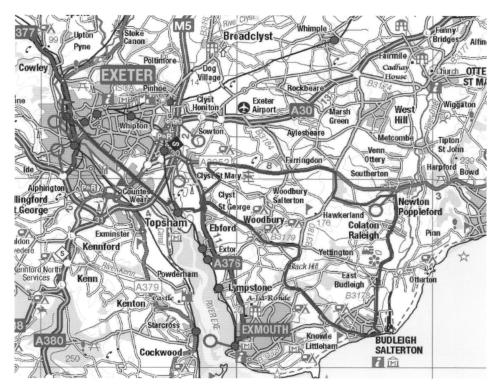

This short loop from Exeter offers a short alternative to the longer rides out on to Dartmoor. There are some fantastic fun and flowing sections of road that lead you out to the coast where you will get a brief glimpse of the sea before heading back inland on some quiet minor roads, passing through picturesque villages and stunning countryside.

From the station head left on the main A377 then switch right. Climbing up St David's Hill, follow straight on through the city centre up Iron Bridge on to North Street, passing along South Street to the main intersection with Holloway Street. Take care crossing the junction and position yourself to take the exit on to Holloway Street on the A3015.

The A3015 runs through the city in a south-easterly direction. Continue straight over at the roundabout and on to a minor road, which will pass over the motorway. Shortly after you need to take a left turn up and over the railway, then make a right turn into the village of Topsham.

*The south Devonshire Coast and a chance to grab refreshments.*

*Grand avenues of trees lead you down to the sea.*

As you leave the village you will pass near the weir and up to the main trunk road. At the roundabout, take a left turn. Within a few metres you will come to another roundabout. Take a right turn on to the B3179. You will follow the road through open countryside, climbing and descending slightly as you head to the village of Woodbury.

The route brings you up to a junction with the B3180 where you need to take a right turn, heading around Blackhill towards Budleigh Salterton. This section of road winds its way through trees and has some interesting movement: small undulations and rhythmic corners are accompanied by a fast, smooth surface.

You will descend down to a roundabout. Head straight over (on to the B3178) into the seaside town of Budleigh Salterton. Here you have the option of following the B road back inland in a northerly direction or adding on a small additional loop along the seafront, which I highly recommend. The road simply follows the seafront for a few hundred metres before switching left while climbing up to rejoin the B3178.

As you head northwards you will pass through East Budleigh with the River Otter running parallel with you on your right. There are no real climbs in this route so

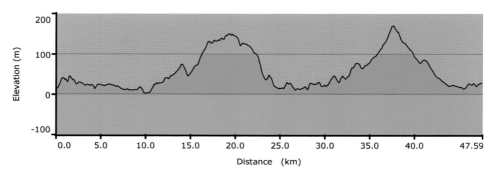

*A footpath to the right provides an alternative to a soaking if the ford is deep.*

enjoy carrying some speed, safe in the knowledge that you're not going to suffer a huge climb later on.

In just over a kilometre outside the village of Colaton Raleigh you will pass a small woodland to your left. Just beyond the wood you need to take a left turn on to a minor road towards Stoneyford village. The lanes leading up to the village are quite narrow. The high hedges make it hard for you to pass any vehicles, however, these lanes are rarely used and make a good alternative to the main A road which runs parallel to the north. It should also be noted that the lanes can become quite mucky due to tractors accessing the fields in and around the area. If you prefer, instead of turning left towards Stoneyford you can simply carry straight on into Newton Poppleford where you come to a T-junction with the main A3052. Here take a left turn and follow the A road.

The narrow country lane brings you up to a T-junction where you will take a right turn on the B3180. In just over a kilometre you come to a junction with the main A3052, where you should take a left-hand turn. In just under seven kilometres you arrive in the village of Clyst St Mary. Just before the village take a left turn into a narrow lane signposted towards Woodbury Salterton.

Another kilometre of fun narrow lanes pass before you need to take a right turn down another narrow lane. You will recognise the junction by the red postbox buried in the hedge and signs for Kenniford farm shop. As you arrive at the village of Clyst St George you need to pass through a small ford. If the ford is running deep there is the option of taking the footpath to the right. Follow the road up into the village centre and bear round to the left. Within a few metres you're back to the B3179, the road you took on your outwardbound route.

To get back to the start point retrace your steps back into Exeter, crossing over the main A376 trunk road. Alternatively swing left for another lap and trip to the sea.

# 6 EXMOOR: MINEHEAD MASH-UP

**Start point:** Minehead railway station

**Grid ref:** SS 97478 46383

**Postcode:** TA24 5SH

**Total distance:** 74km

**Total elevation:** 1544m

**Max elevation:** 440m

## KEY CLIMBS

**From km 0 to km 4:** 115m climb over 4km

**From km 9.5 to km 15.5:** 388m climb over 6km

**From km 28 to km 39:** 416m climb over 11km

**Exposure:** 3/5

*The rugged coastline and rolling road from Minehead.*

This route will take you high up above the cliff tops overlooking the Bristol Channel. Passing through some stunning scenery and coastal villages you will then head inland and climb up through Exmoor National Park, crossing the moor to the village of Exford before dropping down back to the coast.

From the train station pick up The Avenue and head in a westerly direction through the town centre, passing through The Parade on to Parkhouse Road, and continue to follow to the main A39. Here you take a right turn and follow the main A road.

At the village of Porlock the road climbs steeply through the woodland with a series of tight switchbacks. As you crest Porlock Hill the road continues to climb slightly as it traverses parallel to the sea and on to Culbone Hill. You will continue to traverse along a ridge line pass an old Roman fortlet and on to Countisbury Common. From the common you descend

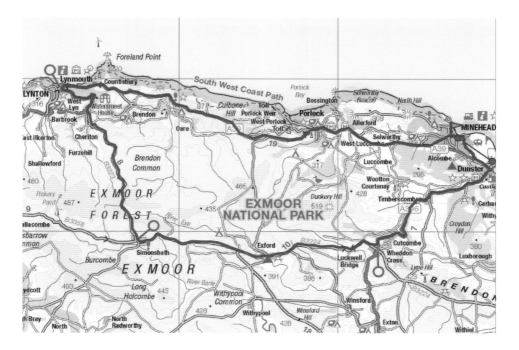

down a steep hill into the villages of Lyn-mouth and Lynton.

The two villages are linked with the cliff-top railway. Although this is not on the route it's worth a small diversion into the village centre to have a look. The route continues to follow the main A road along Lyn Cleave and Myrtleberry Cleave next to the East Lyn River. The steep-sided valley is lined with trees and the road snakes its way uphill to the B3223 on your left.

Follow the B road in a southerly direc-tion, continuing to climb up the valley. This is a reasonable climb and will bring you up on to Brendon Common at 423m. The road continues to climb steadily as you head towards Simonsbath village. Here the road bears left, joining the B32242 towards Exford. In Exford village take a left turn over the stone bridge continuing to follow the B road to Wheddon Cross. You will pass

*A short stiff climb could be hard work after a pub lunch in Exford.*

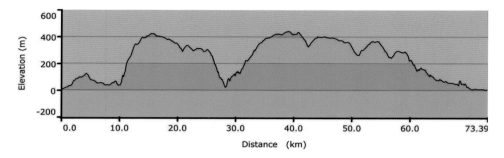

through a steep valley dropping down into Luckwell Bridge and a short steep climb leads you up and over Blagdon Cross before descending into Wheddon Cross.

In the centre of the village take a left turn on to the main A396 towards Timberscombe and Minehead. The section of road leading to Timberscombe twists its way along the valley base. The treelined A road is quite narrow in places and high hedges obscure your visibility. Once in Timberscombe. following the river Avill for a few kilometres back towards the sea, passing through the village of Dunster. Beyond the village you will come to the main A39 where you take a left turn. Within a kilometre you arrive at a roundabout. Here bear right towards the town centre. Just after you cross the railway on to the Strand take a left turn back to the station.

*Heading up on to the moor you finally leave the high hedges behind.*

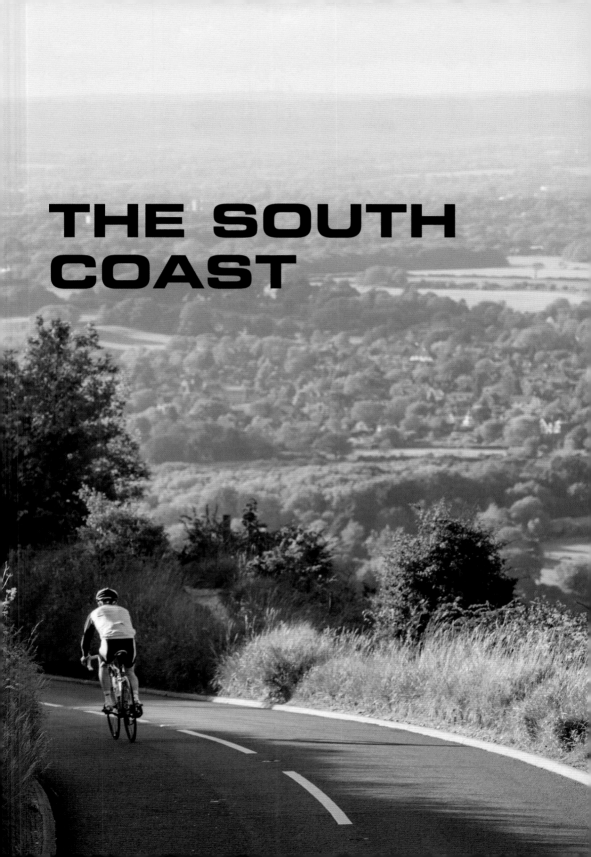

# THE SOUTH COAST

# 7 BRIGHTON AND HOVE 1: DITCHLING DILEMMA

**Start point:** Brighton railway station (London Road)

**Grid ref:** TQ 31324 05759

**Postcode:** BN1 3XP

**Total distance:** 37km

**Total elevation:** 510m

**Max elevation:** 225m

## KEY CLIMBS

**From km 0 to km 9:** 183m climb over 9km

**From km 22.2 to km 27:** 100m climb over 4.8km

**Exposure:** 2.5/5

The well-known seaside resort of Brighton is the start for the next loop. Brighton is steeped in history and was made popular with the Victorian day trippers, thanks to the main rail link with London built in 1841. The seaside town has a host of attractions, including the famous pier

*Brighton Pier.*

and the Grand Hotel, both built by the Victorians. The keen cyclists among you may have participated in the London to Brighton charity bike ride.

If you have previously ridden the London to Brighton bike ride you will be fully aware of Ditchling Beacon. This route is going to send you up on to Ditchling Beacon before dropping down into the village of Ditchling itself. From here traverse along the bottom of the South Downs before climbing back up and over the hills, dropping back down into town. Expect some steep gradients, high speeds and stunning views.

From the London Road station entrance take a left turn along a minor road and another left turn climbing up over the railway heading north. As you climb up out of

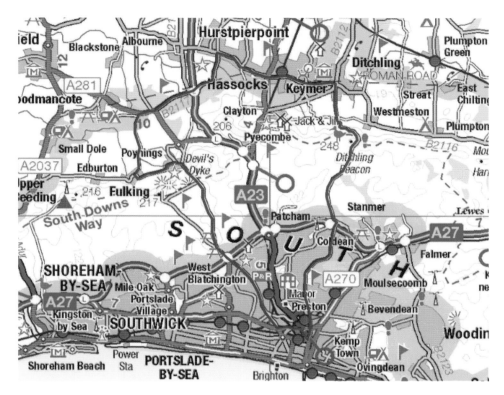

*The narrow and fast descent of Ditchling Beacon.*

the town, the buildings will end and over to your right you will pass the iron age hill fort of Hollingbury Castle.

The road drops down and climbs up. Crossing over the main A27 trunk road, take a left turn and then fork right on to Ditchling Road, climbing up over open ground and heading towards Ditchling Beacon. The descent from Ditchling Beacon down into the village has recently been resurfaced, however, caution should be taken as the road is quite narrow and some of the bends quite tight.

When you arrive in the village take a left turn on to the B2116 towards Hassocks. Pass through Hassocks and continue to Hurstpierpoint. In the centre of the village take a left turn on to the B2117. You will

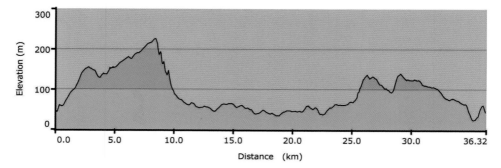

pass over the main trunk road linking to the A281. In just a few hundred metres take a fork left towards Fulking.

Throughout this section you will have stunning views of the South Downs. Your earlier descent of Ditchling Beacon will give you a good idea of the climb ahead that will take you up to Devil's Dyke.

From the village of Fulking take a left turn and traverse open ground before starting to climb up into the treeline. The gradient is quite steep initially. If you get a chance take a look across to your right into Devil's Dyke itself. At the crest of the hill take a right turn as you climb up. You are now running parallel to the South Downs Way.

As you crest the hill, drop down through the golf course into a tight left-hand turn before traversing the hills with views back towards the sea to your right. The route descends back down from the hills, crossing over the major trunk road into Brighton. After a couple of kilometres descending in the built-up area you can pick up signs at a major junction to your left back to London Road station. However, you may want to head down to the seafront for a well-deserved ice cream.

*Climbing up past Devil's Dyke, a rewarding view awaits.*

# 8 BRIGHTON AND HOVE 2: PEACEHAVEN PEDAL

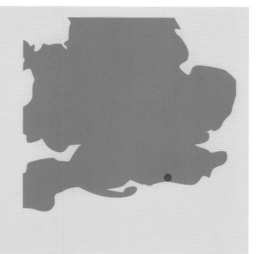

**Start point:** Brighton railway station (London Road)

**Grid ref:** TQ 31324 05759

**Postcode:** BN1 3XP

**Total distance:** 48km

**Total elevation:** 688m

**Max elevation:** 225m

## KEY CLIMBS

**From km 30 to km 40:** 198m climb over 10km

**Exposure:** 2.5/5

The second Brighton loop follows the coast in an easterly direction before heading north and inland back round to the village of Ditchling. This loop will take you up and over the South Downs and bring you back into Brighton via Ditchling Beacon.

From the London Road train station, head southwards following the signs to the seafront. Just before you reach the seafront pick up the B2066 heading east towards Newhaven. This will link you into the main A259 Brighton Road. The road climbs up and drops down several times following the seafront and there are some lovely views out into the channel. The road will drop you into Newhaven where you join the one-way system. Within a few metres the road bears round to the right and you need to head straight on into Lewes Road.

The route follows the road northwards to the town of Lewes with the River Ouse to your right, Here you skirt around the edge of the South Downs and up into the town, crossing over the major trunk road. Follow the minor road over the railway and

*Rolling countryside in the South Downs.*

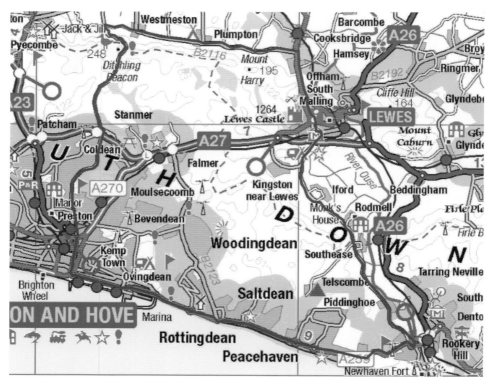

up to a T-junction. Joining the A275, you will then continue to head northwards for a few kilometres before turning left on to the B2116. Just off the route in Lewes town centre is a castle. It's well worth a diversion to go and take a look at this stunning building. You can also take on fuel here and relax before you continue on towards the climb at Ditchling Beacon.

Back on route north of Lewes, take the left turn on to the B2116, heading west towards Ditchling. The road hugs the Downs and skirts its way along the village of Plumpton and onwards to a T-junction with the main Ditchling to Brighton Road. Here take a left turn and start to climb up Ditchling Beacon. The climb has some steep gradients but you do get some rest in between with flatter sections. When

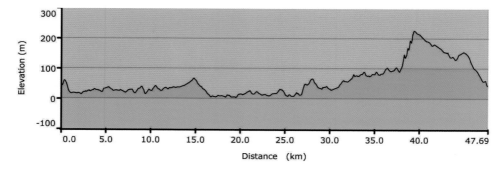

*There is a smooth line somewhere to be found on the rough surface dressing.*

you crest the hill start to traverse across the hilltops before descending down to a T-junction where you take a left turn and then a right, crossing over the major trunk road.

The road then drops down slightly before climbing up, cresting the small hill linking into the final descent back down into Brighton. You will pass over the railway. London Road station is to your right.

*Back down by the seafront in Brighton, a great place to unwind after a ride.*

# 9 SOUTHAMPTON, NEW FOREST 1: BOLDERWOOD BOWL

**Start point:** Southampton Totton railway station

**Grid ref:** SU 36332 13339

**Postcode:** SO40 3AB

**Total distance:** 48km

**Total elevation:** 272m

**Max elevation:** 57m

**Exposure:** 2/5

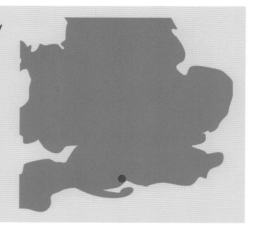

*The lush green surroundings of the New Forest.*

Created by William I as a royal forest around 1080, the New Forest comprises many small hamlets, villages and farmsteads. It is one of the largest remaining unenclosed pastures of heathland and forest within the south. The forest and heathland is home to many animals, from birds of prey such as buzzards and kites to the famous New Forest ponies. This ride will pass through an arboretum with various species of deciduous and non-deciduous trees and takes you out into the heathlands between picturesque villages.

From the town of Totton on the outskirts of Southampton pick up the A336 on the north side of the railway. Follow the A road in a westerly direction, passing over two roundabouts into the village of Netley Marsh. Here the route turns off the busy A road and heads south through Woodlands and into the edge of the New Forest National Park. The narrow lanes twist

their way around on the outskirts of the forest linking into the main A337 Cadnam to Lyndhurst road. You will pass through Goldenhayes village and on past Bentley Manor.

The A337 drops down into the busy town of Lyndhurst. This road can get very busy with queues backing up for a couple of kilometres into the town. It goes without saying to take care when passing stationary traffic – and try to avoid having a smug look on your face as you do so!

Lyndhurst has all the usual amenities and is a good place to stop off for a coffee or snack. The route follows the one-way system through town and continues to head southwards on the A337 towards Brockenhurst. Just before the town, take a left turn and head east towards Beaulieu on the B3055. You will come out of the woodland into open ground across the heathland towards Beaulieu.

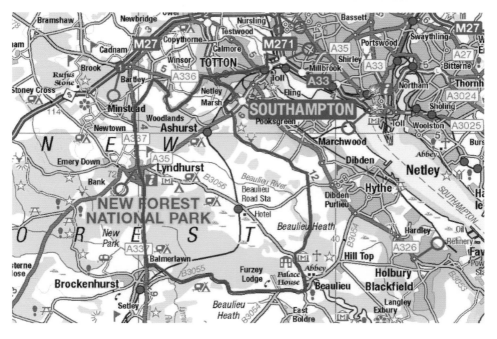

*Quiet lanes pass through picturesque villages on the edge of the forest.*

The B3055 joins into the B3054 at Hatchet a couple of kilometres before Beaulieu. The road swings left on the west side of the village and joins into the B3056 heading north. You will pass the famous National Motor Museum before taking a right turn on to a minor road heading up across Beaulieu Heath.

The road continues for several kilometres and you will pass the New Forest Wildlife Park before entering the village of Ashurst. Take care as you cross over the A35 as you will make a left and then a right turn. This route takes you along some minor roads to avoid a major intersection heading back towards Totton.

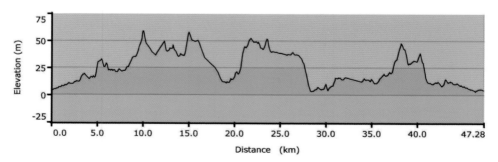

*Horses roam free down in Beaulieu village.*

This short link brings you out on to the A326 and back into Ashurst Bridge. At the roundabout take a right turn to the next roundabout where you rejoin your outward-bound loop. To complete the loop simply retrace your steps back to the railway station.

# 10 SOUTHAMPTON, NEW FOREST 2: BROCKENHURST BASH

**Start point:** Brockenhurst train station

**Grid ref:** SU 30251 02056

**Postcode:** SO42 7UD

**Total distance:** 52km

**Total elevation:** 365m

**Max elevation:** 112m

**Exposure:** 2/5

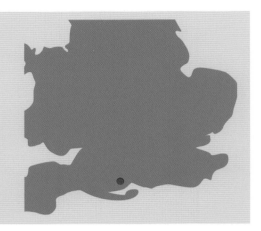

The second New Forest loop starts in the heart of the forest in the town of Brockenhurst. This route takes in the Bolderwood Arboretum Ornamental Drive and passes through stunning woodland and heath-

*The forest drive has some great sequences of corners.*

land as you navigate a lap of the National Forest.

From Brockenhurst head east towards Beaulieu on the B3055. As the previous loop, this road joins into the B3054 at Hatchet and swings left, heading north past the village of Beaulieu before joining into the B3056. Continue on the B road up past the motor museum heading in a north-westerly direction and cutting in and out of the forest towards Beaulieu Road station (you could also start your ride from this location).

The road will eventually bring you into Lyndhurst. The town has all the usual amenities and is a good place to stop off for a coffee or snack. The route follows the one-way system around town and picks up the A35 towards Christchurch. Just outside the town take a fork to the right into a minor road signposted for Emery Down.

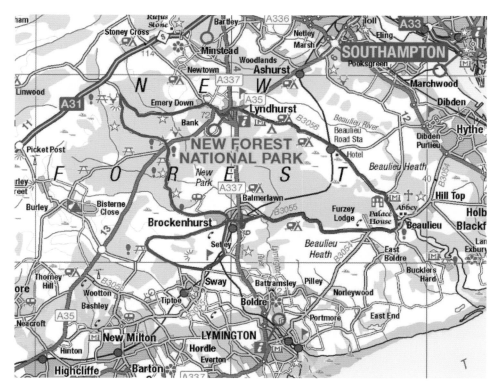

A short climb past some pretty thatched cottages takes you up over a cattle grid into the village. Just after the pub on your left take the fork off to the left and head out into the forest.

The quiet roads around the forest have an enchanting feel to them. The 40mph speed limit means that any vehicles you do come across should be travelling relatively slowly. After several kilometres you will see signs on your left for the Bolderwood Arboretum Ornamental Drive. Take a switch-back to the left and join the scenic drive.

The scenic drive really is a stunning piece of road. The asphalt snakes its way through various species of trees, and giant pines tower above as you head back towards the main A road. Take care when

*There are some great buildings in the forest.*

crossing the main road and continue to follow the Forest Drive on the opposite side, heading in a southerly direction.

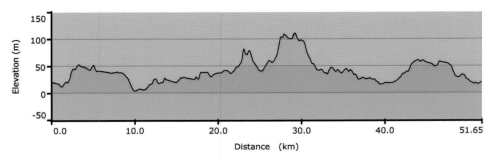

*With minimal elevation change you can let rip on the short hills.*

You will pass by the Rhinefield House Hotel. Built in 1887 this spectacular building boasts both Tudor- and Gothic-style architecture. If you're feeling flush you may wish to stop off for a light bite. The road continues to make its way through the forest back to the town of Brockenhurst. Here you have the option to end your ride or head back out into the forest for one final loop. Simply continue round to the right and head out of town in a westerly direction past Five Thorns Hill out on to Hincheslea Moor.

This additional loop has some great views and is a worthy addition to the ride. The road swings round to the left, heading back along Long Slade Bottom before coming to a T-junction with the B3055. Simply take a left turn and follow the road for a few kilometres back into Brockenhurst.

*Rhinefield House Hotel in the heart of the forest.*

# THE SOUTH, CHILTERN HILLS

# 11 TRING 1: CHILTERN CLASSICS

**Start point:** Tring railway station

**Grid ref:** SP 95047 12251

**Postcode:** HP23 5QR

**Total distance:** 53.8km

**Total elevation:** 717m

**Max elevation:** 247m

## KEY CLIMBS

**From km 1.5 to km 2.6:** 70m climb over 1.1km

**From km 11.9 to km 13.5:** 98m climb over 1.6km

**From km 34.8 to km 45.8:** 162m climb over 11km

**Exposure:** 2/5

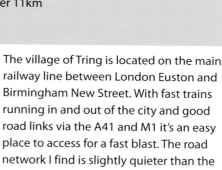

The village of Tring is located on the edge of the Ashridge Estate nestled in the Chiltern Hills. Owned by the National Trust, the estate covers some 5000 acres. and is home to the Ashridge Business School.

*The climb up around Ivinghoe Beacon was often used in the Milk Race Tour of Britain.*

The village of Tring is located on the main railway line between London Euston and Birmingham New Street. With fast trains running in and out of the city and good road links via the A41 and M1 it's an easy place to access for a fast blast. The road network I find is slightly quieter than the options from central London but the hills are a little smaller.

This ride will lead you out through the picturesque village of Aldbury up into the Ashridge Estate and across to Dunstable Downs via Whipsnade Zoo. You will then descend on to the edge of Aylesbury Vale, cutting through small villages and back towards Ivinghoe. Here you start to ascend Ivinghoe Beacon, a road frequently used in the Tour of Britain and local classics.

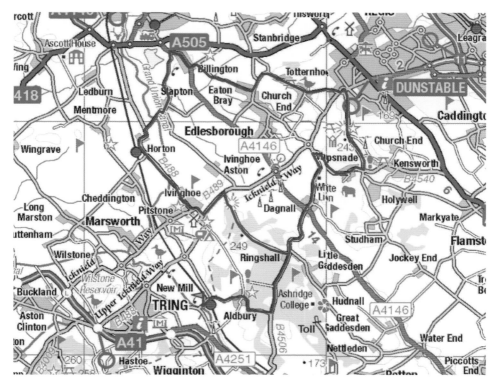

Tring railway station is located to the east of the town. From here head in an easterly direction up and over a small hill into the village of Aldbury. Continue straight through the village and up Toms Hill. This short sharp hill leads you out on to a straight section to a T-junction with the B4506.

*Aldbury village has a well-stocked shop as well as the old stocks.*

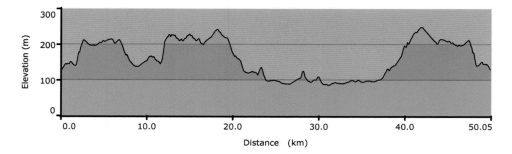

The route then swings left and heads through the Ashridge Estate to the village of Ringshall. Beyond the village, descend down a rough narrow road out of the woods and into open farmland to the A4146. You then cross over the roundabout and pass along the undulating road below Whipsnade Down. You may have noticed the white lion that dons the hillside below the zoo from the descent into Dagnall. The road runs below the lion to a junction on your right, which takes you up Bison Hill past the zoo towards the village of Kensworth on the B4540.

The fast-rolling asphalt dips down and climbs up a couple of times passing the Tree Cathedral to your left at Whipsnade Common before coming to a roundabout. Here take a left turn and climb upwards to the top of Dunstable Downs. As you cross the top of the downs there are some superb views out across Aylesbury Vale and back over to Ivinghoe Beacon.

A fast descent brings you into the outskirts of Dunstable. At the bottom take a left turn at the mini-roundabout and continue a short distance until you meet another. At this second mini-roundabout take a right onto Totternhoe Road, descending down into the village of Totternhoe. The road narrows and passes underneath Totternhoe Knoll before a

short decent drops to a turning on the left signposted towards Eaton Bray. Take this left turn and head towards Eaton Bray and Edlesborough. As you enter the village the route takes a right turn signposted towards Billington.

Join the main A4146 in the village of Billington, taking a right turn and climbing up and over a small but steep hill before descending down through the village. A minor road to your left links through Little Billington and on towards the village of Slapton. Here you have the option to take a shortcut towards Ivinghoe Beacon by taking a left turn towards Ivinghoe Aston.

As you exit the village of Slapton you will pass over the Grand Union Canal and come to a T-junction with the B488. At the T-junction the route takes a left turn heading towards the village of Ivinghoe.

## The Great Train Robber

If you take a right turn heading towards Leighton Buzzard you can see the bridge where the infamous Great Train Robbery (1963) took place. The robbery was the largest of its kind with a heist of £2.6 million (equivalent to £42 million in today's money) in used bank notes. The robbers humped the money sacks down the railway embankment at this bridge into vans

*The classic climb up around Ivinghoe Beacon.*

before driving to the hideout at a nearby airfield; the robbery has only been topped by the Brink's-MAT Robbery in 1983.

The site is nothing spectacular but it is of historical interest. If you wish to see the bridge it is just off the first turning to your left as you head northwards on the B488 towards Leighton Buzzard.

The route takes a left turn heading in a southerly direction through the village of Horton and onwards towards Ivinghoe. You will pass back over the Grand Union Canal once more before coming into the village. In Ivinghoe take a left turn and shortly after exiting the village take

another left turn and start the steady climb on the B489 towards Ivinghoe Beacon. As you approach the beacon on your right-hand side, take a right turn and climb up the hillside past the beacon and on to Ivinghoe Hill. You will climb up through the S bend where you get a great view back across to Dunstable Downs and Whipsnade Zoo. The road continues to climb back into the Ashridge Estate before descending down into Ringshall. From here simply retrace your steps and enjoy the fast descent down Toms Hill back through Aldbury and on to the railway station at Tring where you started the ride.

# 12 TRING 2: A PLAYBOY'S PLAYGROUND

**Start point:** Tring railway station

**Grid ref:** SP 95047 12251

**Postcode:** HP23 5QR

**Total distance:** 40km

**Total elevation:** 512m

**Max elevation:** 247m

## KEY CLIMBS

**From km 5.5 to km 9.5:** 124m climb over 4km

**From km 21.5 to km 22.5:** 64m climb over 1km

**From km 31.2 to km 34.2:** 76m climb over 3km

**Exposure:** 2/5

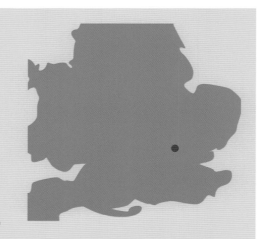

*A fast descent on the quiet lanes and some challenging corners.*

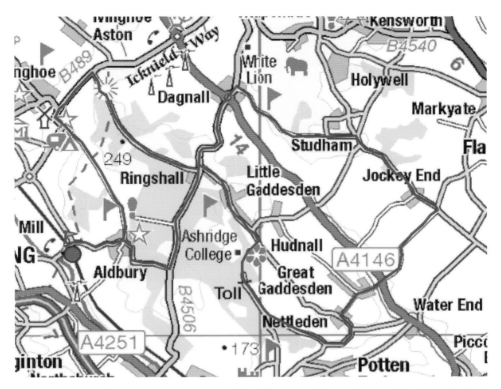

The second loop from Tring is a variation of the first. It will take you through picturesque countryside, hooking up some great climbs and fast descents. On this loop you will get a different view of the Chiltern Hills from the previous route and take in the classic Ivinghoe Beacon climb once more before heading off past a spectacular building that is now home to a business school within the Ashridge Estate and continue on to Jockey End and Gaddesden Row. The ride then swings back behind Whipsnade Zoo, crossing the valley and up into the Ashridge Estate, returning to the railway station via Toms Hill.

From the station, head east towards the village of Aldbury. By the pond and stocks in the village centre take a left turn and head up the narrow lane in a northerly direction. The road passes Stocks Golf Club. The large manor house you will see on your left-hand side used to belong to the infamous Playboy millionaire Hugh Hefner.

*The idyllic village pond in Aldbury.*

The road narrows and starts to climb up before crossing the Ridgeway path at Pitstone Hill. This section of road formed part of the original Icknield Way Path.

A short but steep fast descent will bring you down to a junction with the B488. Continue straight down, passing the windmill through the S bends to a junction on your right with the B489. This is the start of the climb up towards Ivinghoe Beacon, which was used many years ago in 'The Milk Race', aka Tour of Britain. As you approach the Beacon take the turning on your right-hand side and continue to climb up on to Ivinghoe Hill. Here are some stunning views across towards Dunstable Downs and the surrounding Chiltern Hills.

As you enter the Ashridge Estate heading towards the village of Ringshall, the road passes through some ancient woodland. At the T-junction take a left turn, climb up the short rise and then take a right turn towards Little Gaddesden. Pass through the village and take a right fork into the private drive for the business school. The road descends down over a series of speed ramps before climbing up and passing in front of the magnificent building, which was featured in the film *The Dirty Dozen* (1967), standing in for the chateau in Germany that was attacked by the Dirty Dozen near the end of the movie.

The road continues past the college and descends down through Berkhamsted Common. Just before the road starts to climb again take a left turn towards Frithsden. The narrow lane runs along the bottom of the hill with woodland up to your right. At the end of the lane, pass the pub and come to a T-junction where you need to take a left turn descending towards Nettleden.

In Nettleden village take a right turn and drop downhill. At the bottom of the

*Smooth rolling roads in the Chilterns.*

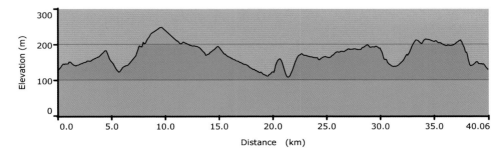

hill you cross the River Gade before crossing the main A4146. The road then climbs
uphill and towards Gaddesden Row. A left
turn will take you to Jockey End and on
to Clement's End. Keep right and follow
the road ahead towards Studham. Just
after you enter the village take a left at the
crossroads towards Dagnall.

The narrow road snakes its way along
the hilltops before descending. The hedges
are high and there is little room for passing should you meet oncoming traffic so
take care as you head down towards the
village of Dagnall. When you arrive in the
village take a left at the T-junction and roll
through the village to the roundabout.
Here the route heads straight over before
climbing back up into the Ashridge Estate,
passing back through the village of Ringshall. At the time of writing, the surface up
to the village wasn't particularly great.

Having passed through Ringshall
continue to follow the road through the
woodland. You will see an entrance to your
right which takes you up to a monument
where you will find a small cafe should you
wish to have a break for refreshments. This
main drive also links in the opposite direction to the business school but you would
need a bike suitable for off-road in order
to get there. The route continues past this
entrance and on to a right turn signposted
for Aldbury and Tring.

At the end of the long straight the road
swings down to the left into a switchback
right before descending Toms Hill. It's
easy to hit some high speeds down here
but take care when you come into the
30mph limit as the road swings round a
left-hand corner and there are sometimes
parked cars in this area. You will pass back
through the village where you headed on
your outward-bound route. You can either
continue back to the railway station or turn
right for a second lap.

# 13 WENDOVER 1 : GREAT MISSENDEN MISSION

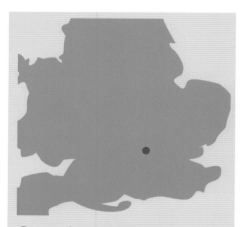

**Start point:** Wendover railway station

**Grid ref:** SP 86558 07757

**Postcode:** HP22 6BT

**Total distance:** 54km

**Total elevation:** 914m

**Max elevation:** 263m

## KEY CLIMBS

**From km 0 to km 4.2:** 106m climb over 4.2km

**From km 10 to km 13.5:** 101m climb over 3.5km

**From km 19 to km 22.2:** 125m climb over 3.2km

**From km 30 to km 40:** 118m climb over 10km

**From km 44.2 to km 48.2:** 136m climb over 4km

**Exposure:** 2/5

*Arable farmland and ancient woodland. The Chilterns hide many picturesque scenes.*

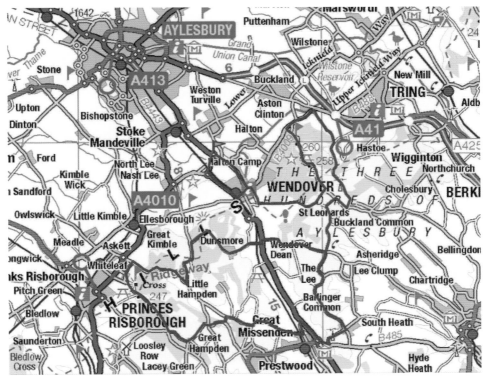

This ride starts from the small village of Wendover, which is easily accessed by rail and road. The loop takes you up and around Wendover Woods. Climbing up via Aston Hill, you will then cycle towards Princes Risborough, passing Chequers, country home of the Prime Minister. There are some steep climbs that lead you back up on to the hills before a fleeting visit to the quaint village of Great Missenden. Back on the east side of the main A413 trunk road the route heads northwards along the hilltops before descending into Wendover. This route has some fantastic views as you pass through many quaint villages nestled in the Chiltern Hills.

From the railway station the ride starts by taking a left turn and dropping down towards the high street. Take a right turn at the mini-roundabout and head out of town towards the A413. Just outside the built-up area take a left turn, dropping down around the church before switching back to the left and climbing uphill slightly. Take a right turn. The road now heads in an easterly direction along a straight climb to The Hail. The gradient steepens up as you pass through Hale Wood and on towards the village of St Leonards.

Beyond Sunderland's village the route then heads in a northerly direction down the narrow lanes to a steep descent at The Crong. Take care through the next section as the road is narrow and the hedges high. Beyond The Crong, take a left turn towards Aston Clinton. This section of road is known locally as Gravity Hill, and there are many stories relating to ghosts of

*The narrow lanes in the Chilterns are quite rough and dirty.*

dead motorists assisting other motorists to pass over the hill. Rather than ghosts, however, this is an optical illusion but it's worth stopping and playing with Gravity Hill. The section of road I'm referring to is a small rise before the long straight descent. As you round the slight right-hand corner past the house on the right it appears that the road runs uphill slightly. Stop here at the bottom and then let the brakes off, you will 'magically' roll uphill.

At the bottom of Gravity Hill take a left turn, picking up the B4009 signposted back towards Wendover. This is the start of a relatively long climb for the area, and you will fork off left up into Wendover Woods climbing Aston Hill. Beyond Aston Hill the road drops down into the village of Chivery. Take a right turn here, then a left. Following a section of road you took on you outward-bound loop, after a short distance fork off to the right heading towards Lee Gate and Swan Bottom.

The route takes a right turn in Lee Gate and passes over the hilltops before descending through some nice flowing corners to the main A413. Take care when crossing the main road and get ready for another short steep gradient on the other side leading up into the small hamlet of Dunsmore, As you crest the hill through Dunsmore you will drop down a very steep gradient. Take care here particularly in the wet as the road is off-camber!

The road then descends down to a T-junction at Lodge Hill where you head in a southerly direction, passing Chequers. Just over a kilometre past Chequers take a right turn climbing up through the woodland towards Lower Cadsden. To your right in the woodland lies an ancient hill fort, you would have also crossed over the Ridgeway Path a few times by this point.

Before you reach the main road, pick up a narrow lane on your left-hand side cutting below Whiteleaf village. At the

*Rolling hills, open fields and ancient woodlands, a great mix for a great ride.*

T-junction take a left turn, climbing up a steep gradient through the woods up into open ground. A fast descent on the other side takes you down to Redlands End. Swing left and head towards the village of Great Hampden.

Passing Great Hampden and then pass through Hampden Bottom and descend into the village of Great Missenden. The route passes through the bottom of the valley crossing the main A413 once more before a steep climb brings you back on to the hilltops. Swing left, heading northwards back towards The Lee. Here simply retrace your steps and descend back through Hale Wood and down into Wendover.

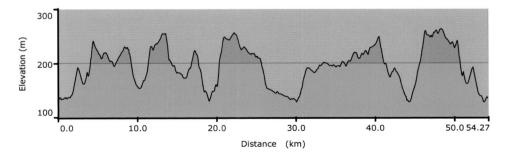

# 14 WENDOVER 2: LUDGERSHALL LOOP

**Start point:** Wendover railway station

**Grid ref:** SP 86558 07757

**Postcode:** HP22 6BT

**Total distance:** 75km

**Total elevation:** 700m

**Max elevation:** 190m

## KEY CLIMBS

**From km 19 to km 30:** 122m climb over 11km

**From km 48 to km 51:** 66m climb over 3km

**From km 56 to km 73:** 106m climb over 17km

**Exposure:** 2/5

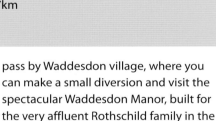

This loop takes you away from the Chiltern Hills out across Aylesbury Vale, where you will be treated to spectacular views. The route passes the railway centre at Quainton, where enthusiasts maintain and run steam locomotives. You will also

*Curling into the Vale of Aylesbury.*

pass by Waddesdon village, where you can make a small diversion and visit the spectacular Waddesdon Manor, built for the very affluent Rothschild family in the late nineteenth century.

From the railway station take a right turn and climb up the hill towards the village of Butler's Cross. Follow the undulating road through Ellesborough to the main A4010 and turn left up the small rise into Great Kimble. On the crest of the hill by the pub take a right turn. Take care when crossing over as this road can be quite busy at times.

The country lane crosses the railway tracks before swinging left on to the B4009 towards Longwick. Just beyond Meadle, take a right turn heading towards the

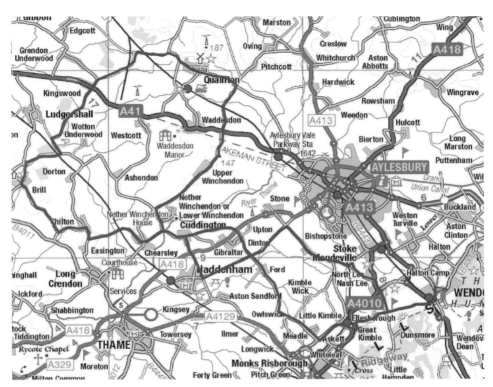

villages Little Meadle and Ford. You will eventually come to the main A418 where you cross straight over heading to the village of Cuddington. The route passes through Cuddington and on to the village of Chearsley. Here in Chearsley bear right and follow the winding lanes towards Chilton.

The route then will take you in a northerly direction heading up to Brill. A short but tough climb leads up into the village where a fast descent will drop you down to a crossroads. Take a right turn and continue to descend past Rushbeds Wood. Just after the railway take a left turn and pass through the wood along a narrow lane to the junction on your right. Take this right turn and continue with woodland on your right-hand side.

The narrow lane takes you back towards the Roman road of Akerman Street. This now forms a section of the A41 trunk road

*The windmill on Brill Hill looks out over the Vale of Aylesbury and can be seen from miles around.*

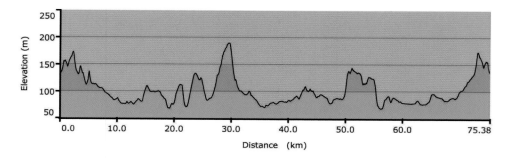

linking Aylesbury to Bicester. Take care crossing the road and continue on minor roads past Kingswood before forking right across open ground. Passing through Shipton Lee the route swings right towards Quainton. If you wish to visit the railway centre take a right turn from the village centre and follow the road for just over one kilometre.

The route however continues straight through the village and on to a crossroads where you will take a right turn and head

*Waddesdon Manor in all its splendour.*

in a southerly direction back towards the A41, Akerman Street. You will now be on the east side of Waddesdon village. If you wish to visit the splendid chateaux-esque Manor, take a right turn and follow the main road into the village where you will pick up signs. The route, however, crosses the staggered junction and climbs up on to Waddesdon Hill. A fine section of rolling road lies before you as you make your way across the hilltops towards Upper Winchendon. A few kilometres past the village take a left turn at a small crossroads and drop back down towards the village of Cuddington. Down in the village the route takes a right turn heading southwards, crossing over the A418 and on to Haddenham.

Swing left and head back towards Aylesbury. Taking a right turn at the village of Stone back towards Butler's Cross, you will pass over and follow for a short section the A4010 by North Lee village. The final leg from Butler's Cross runs along the bottom of Coombe Hill and Bacombe Hill back into the village of Wendover.

# THE
# MIDLANDS,
# COTSWOLDS

# 15 BANBURY 1: SHAKESPEARE'S WORLD

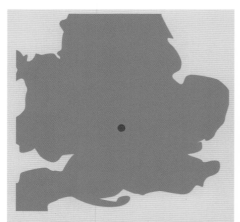

**Start point:** Banbury railway station

**Grid ref:** SP 46158 40426

**Postcode:** OX16 5AB

**Total distance:** 82km

**Total elevation:** 750m

**Max elevation:** 215m

## KEY CLIMBS

**From km 0 to km 13:** 120m climb over 13km

**From km 64 to km 68:** 106m climb over 4km

**Other key elevation gain:** From km 35 to km 68: elevation gain of 175m over 33km

**Exposure:** 2.5/5

*Banbury town centre.*

The town Banbury dates back to the late fifth century and is located on the River Cherwell. The area is relatively low lying and flat. It's often windy in this area, so on the outbound sections this could make for hard work as there is little shelter. On the return leg, some of the rolling hills are also exposed but here

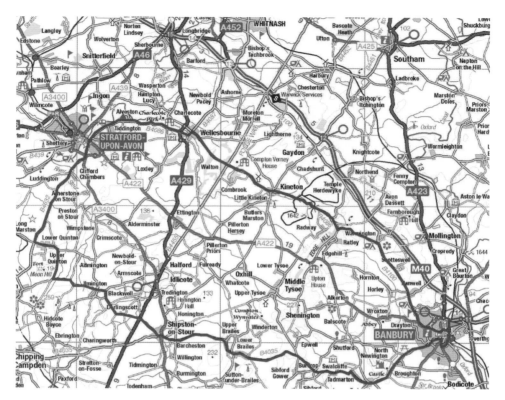

the hedgerows provide a little protection.

The ride starts in the town centre at the railway station. You can navigate your way through the town centre one of several ways. The traffic can get quite heavy at peak times and weekends so caution should be taken on the junctions and roundabouts. If you head north from the station with the railway line on your right you will come to a roundabout. Turn left and follow round a left turn to another roundabout where you take a right. This will put you on the A442 heading out of town towards the west.

As the built-up area thins out you take a right turn just before Drayton school on to the B4100. The opening section is easy-going as you head out towards the village

of Warmington. Just before the village you will see the National Herb Centre on your right.

From Warmington the route bears left on to the B4086 to Knowle End and Edge Hill. The road has some nice move-

*Be careful not to miss the left turn to Edge Hill.*

*The splendid Compton Verney House.*

ment and the surface is relatively good. At Knowle End bear right and drop down a fast descent through the trees and out into open ground, beyond the descent lies the village of Kineton, here the road swings left in front of the church.

The scenery changes and becomes more undulating. Just before you cross over the Fosse Way Roman road you will see Compton Verney House to your right. The mansion house was built in 1714 and is now an art gallery surrounded by ornamental lakes. It's a stunning place to stop and take a break.

The route crosses the Fosse Way and heads into Wellesbourne where you take a left turn in the village centre. Cross the river before taking a right on the B4086 and continue towards Stratford-upon-Avon. Within a few kilometres you enter the outskirts of Stratford-upon-Avon – the giveaway that you're there will be the sizable houses and chic motorcars.

In the town you will have the main River Avon to your right. If you fancy taking a break in town, take a right turn over the bridge and enter the picturesque town centre. This route avoids the town centre by taking a left on to the roundabout then forking off to the right in-front of the petrol station on the A3400. Just after a second roundabout, fork right on to the B4632. A few kilometres later you will pass Long Marston Airfield where you need to

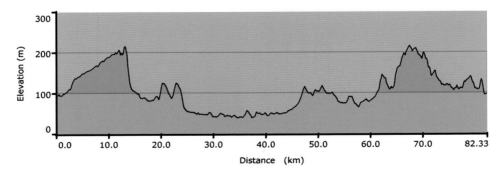

*The historical town centre lies just over the River Avon.*

take a left turn to Lower Quinton. You will now be on minor roads that twist and turn between high hedges.

From Lower Quinton follow the blue Sustrans signs to Ilmington and on to Darlingscott. You will approach the Fosse Way once more. Take care as you cross straight over. Continue on minor roads into Shipston-on-Stour. Here the route joins the B4035 and passes through the village centre. Head over the River Stour on the B road in an easterly direction towards Upper and Lower Brailes.

The climb up Fant Hill into Upper Brailes is reasonably steep and if you have spent too much energy on your outbound section could be quite arduous. The road back to Banbury is full of undulations so it's worth saving some energy for this section.

The B4035 leads you back into Banbury. Follow your nose and head on into the town centre. To complete the loop, at the second roundabout with the famous Banbury Cross take a right then a left back towards the railway station.

*The busy Fosse Way is well signposted.*

# 16 BANBURY 2: TWO-STROKE BLUES

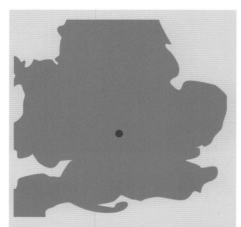

**Start point:** Banbury railway station

**Grid ref:** SP 46158 40426

**Postcode:** OX16 5AB

**Total distance:** 48km

**Total elevation:** 517m

**Max elevation:** 222m

## KEY CLIMBS

**From km 16.4 to km 19.5:** 105m climb over 3.1km

**Other key elevation gain:** From km 0 to km 19.5: elevation gain of 129m over 19.5km

**Exposure:** 2.5/5

*Banbury cross.*

This shorter loop takes in some interesting narrow lanes that undulate and twist their way around the many villages to the west of Banbury. There are some wonderful views of the surrounding countryside and the small picturesque villages are full of delightful cottages made from the local sandstone and donned with thatched roofs. I used to race karts over at Shenington when I was in my youth, so this ride for me is a real blast from the past.

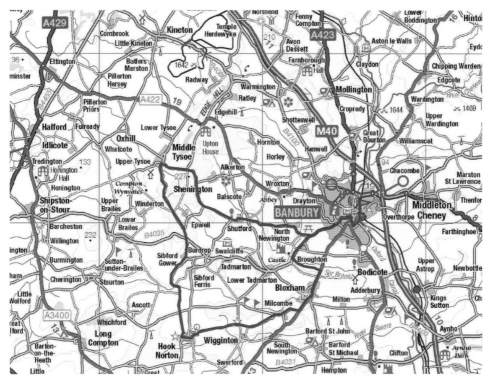

From the railway station make your way around the southern side of the town centre on the A4260. Take a right turn on the B4100 and drop down through a set of traffic lights towards The Cross. Here you take a left turn on to the B4035. Head west out of town.

Just past The Bretch picnic spots take a right turn towards North Newington

following the minor road to the village of Shutford. As you leave the village you will pass Long Hill on your left-hand side as you climb up towards the village of Shenington. Here in Shenington you will see the gliding club and kart racing track on your right-hand side. If there is a race weekend on you will smell the two-stroke oil and hear the buzzing of these high-powered

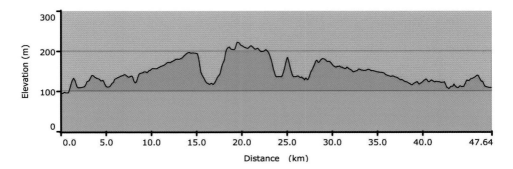

*Trees line lanes that link open countryside.*

machines. It's worth dropping in to watch some spectacular wheel-to-wheel racing.

The road swings left around Shentow Hill and after the crossroads drops down the short steep gradient of Tysoe Hill into Middle Tysoe village. Here you have some spectacular views as you descend down between the hedgerows before passing through open farmland into the village. From the village take a left turn and head in a southerly direction climbing up Lady Elizabeth's Hill.

The narrow lane winds its way south-wards back towards the B4035. The road has some nice movement and the hedges provide shelter but unfortunately obscure the views of oncoming traffic, so take care. Follow the B road back through Swalcliffe village towards Banbury. When you arrive back in the town simply retrace your steps to the railway station.

# THE WELSH BORDERS

# 17 HEREFORD 1: BLACK MOUNTAIN BLAST

**Start point:** Hereford railway station

**Grid ref:** SO51524 40522

**Postcode:** HR1 1BB

**Total distance:** 146km

**Total elevation:** 1733m

**Max elevation:** 564m

## KEY CLIMBS

**From km 71 to km 73.3:** 135m of climb over 2.3km

**From km 83 to km 101:** 417m of climb over 18km

**Exposure:** 4.5/5

This epic loop starting from Hereford will take you way up the Golden Valley to the literary town of Hay-on-Wye before circling around the outskirts of the Black Mountains towards Abergavenny. The ride then heads northwards through the heart of the Black Mountains, passing through the Vale of Ewyas and up over Gospel Pass. An epic descent will brings you back down into the town of Hay-on-Wye and a scenic stroll through the countryside leads back to Hereford.

From the railway station pick up the main A465 and take a right turn towards the town centre. You will come to a major junction where you need to take a right turn and follow the inner ring road around the north side of the town centre. This leads you to a roundabout where you take a left turn signposted towards Abergavenny. The road passes over the river and can get quite busy at peak times. As you pass over the river you need to position yourself in the right-hand lane ready for the next junction where you take a right turn on to the A465 signposted towards Abergavenny.

Within a few kilometres the road rises up out of town passing Belmont Abbey to your right. Beyond the small coppice take a right fork on to the B4349, which is clearly signposted towards Hay-on-Wye. The opening section of road that leads you out to Hay is relatively flat; you pass through fantastic countryside with little evidence of what lies in store. It's worth saving some energy through these opening sections as there are some tough climbs ahead.

In the village of Clehonger take a fork to the left continuing along the B4349. You will pass through some quaint villages as you follow along the Golden Valley. A flowing descent lead you down to a T-junction with the B352 heading down into Hay-on-Wye.

Down in Hay you will come to a T-junction where you need to take a left turn. You will now be heading in a westerly direction. Just outside the built-up area you have the option of leaving the major road and joining a side road to your left towards Llanigon village. I highly recommend doing this as the lane has a great surface. Visibility is also good and it generally has a better feel than following the main road.

The winding lane follows a Sustrans route and avoids the busy trunk road. It

*The Golden Valley looking slightly less golden. On a nice day it's a splendid place to roll along.*

will link you on to the quieter A4078 and into the village of Talgarth. Just outside the village are the remains of an old castle. If you wish to take a look, take a right turn on the main A479 trunk road and within several hundred metres you can see the castle on your right-hand side. The route

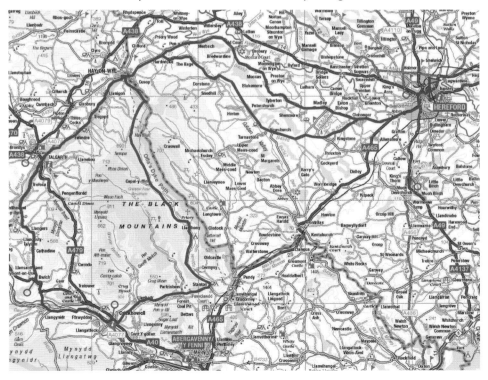

joins the trunk road after taking a left turn and follows it for a few metres before forking off to the right at a roundabout that takes you on to B4560, towards Trefecca village.

The road now starts to throw some larger undulations at you as you navigate your way around the Black Mountains. To your left there are some spectacular views along this section of road as you pass Llangors Lake. The village of Llangors is an ideal place to stop and take on some fuel before you head off into the mountains.

The B road winds its way down to the main A40 trunk road, which you will join for a short distance. When you come to the village of Bwlch, take a left turn and climb up into the village before descending through a right-hand switchback and down a fast section of road to a tight left-hand corner. Before the corner position yourself on the road in preparation to make a right turn for the B4560 into Llangynidr Bridge. You can't miss the junction as there are signs warning large goods vehicles about the width restrictions for the bridge further down.

*The beautiful stone bridge over the River Usk.*

A steep descent drops you down to the bridge. After you cross over the River Usk, climb up a steep gradient on the other side to a T-junction. Take a left turn here and cycle in an easterly direction along the B4558. This is a very picturesque section of road and you will run parallel to the Monmouthshire and Brecon Canal.

The B road brings you into the village of Ffawyddog where you should take a left turn. Crossing back over the river and up to the main A40 trunk road, take a right

*Passing through Llangors village and around the mountains.*

*The long narrow lane leads you up the valley to the main climb.*

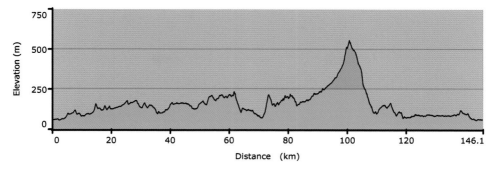

and follow for a few metres before a left turn. The turn is located just after a pelican crossing and is signposted towards a car park. Climb up for a couple of hundred metres to a mini-roundabout. This section can seem quite vague due to the lack of signage. At the mini-roundabout take a right turn and continue to climb uphill out of the village.

The road narrows and hugs the hillside as you climb up on to the edge of the Black Mountains. Throughout this section you will climb up and descend several times as you head towards the village of Stanton. The route takes a left turn, heading northwards with the River Affon Honddu running parallel on your right. Continue to follow the narrow lane (which can become dirty in the wet season) up into the mountains.

The lane is very narrow and will lead you uphill into a steep climb over Gospel Pass. A cattle grid on the climb can present an interesting challenge on a wet day!

As you crest the hill you have spectacular views of the Welsh borders. A fresh ribbon of asphalt stretches out ahead of you as you descend across open hilltops back down towards Hay-on-Wye. The gradient gets quite steep in places and you have to cross over another cattle grid,

*The superb smooth narrow road winding its way through the mountains, a fast descent to Hay-on-Wye awaits.*

so take care when descending. The road is also very narrow and there is little room for passing vehicles.

Back in Hay take a right turn into the town centre and another right turn where you headed out from earlier. You now have the option of retracing your steps or following the B4352 back to Hereford. If you follow this route, the remaining kilometres are relatively easy-going with small undulations and no major climbs.

# 18 HEREFORD 2: LITERARY LOOP

**Start point:** Hereford railway station

**Grid ref:** SO51524 40522

**Postcode:** HR1 1BB

**Total distance:** 64km

**Total elevation:** 542m

**Max elevation:** 174m

**Key elevation gain:** From km 0 to km 25: elevation gain of 116m over 25km

**Exposure:** 2.5/5

A short yet scenic loop takes you out along the Golden Valley to Hay-on-Wye. The small town is steeped in history and is home to two castles, one of which dominates the town centre and dates back to Norman times. The small but busy town is filled with book and antique stores and is home to the famous literary festival that each year attracts visitors from across the globe.

The shorter loop simply follows the same outward-bound route as loop one. If you wish to do so you can divert down into Hay-on-Wye or simply take a right turn picking up the B4352 back round towards Hereford.

This shorter loop offers you a fast blast if you're limited on time or if the weather out in the mountains is looking less savoury. Scattered all around this loop are sites of scientific and archaeological interest, from the motte and bailey at

*Hay High Street.*

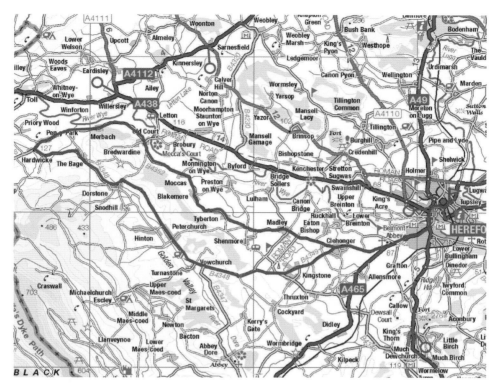

*Deciduous trees on the roadside along the Golden Valley.*

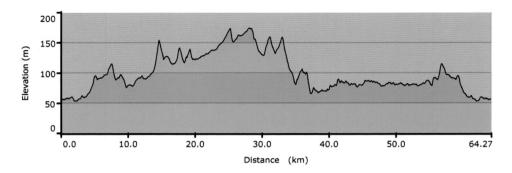

Monnington Court to the burial chamber at Arthur's Stone. There is another motte and bailey at Dorstone village, further evidence that this area has been inhabited and fought over for many years.

Along the route you also get spectacular views of the River Wye as you make your return leg passing Westonhill Wood and Moccas Deer Park.

There are a cluster of narrow lanes in and around the area and with the use of a good GPS device or Ordnance Survey map you can ride to your heart's content.

*Rolling hillsides hide the archeological remains of the great Roman Empire.*

# 19 CHURCH STRETTON 1: THE STING

**Start point:** Church Stretton railway station

**Grid ref:** SO 45529 93605

**Postcode:** SY6 6PG

**Total distance:** 104km

**Total elevation:** 1572m

**Max elevation:** 492m

## KEY CLIMBS

**From km 24 to km 56:** 328m climb over 32km

**From km 74.5 to km 81:** 107m climb over 6.5km

**From km 89 to km 98:** 329m climb over 9km

**Exposure:** 4/5

The first of two loops from Church Stretton railway station is a real epic. The ride starts by passing through Ape Dale and climbing over Wenlock Edge, the route then heads westwards through Craven Arms and out to the town of Clun. You will pass the ruins of Clun Castle and continue west, circum-navigating around Clun Forest. At the most westerly point of this route, you will cross the border into Wales and pick up some spectacular views of the Welsh mountains before entering a superb downhill. The route then makes its return leg heading east, passing near the town of Mont-gomery before crossing the border to the town of Bishop's Castle. The final sting in the tail is a quick up and over the Long Mynd, a spectacular range of hills with some stunning views and challenging asphalt.

From the railway station head east, crossing the major A49 trunk road (and Roman road) and picking up the B4371.

*The Sting in the tail! A tough climb up onto the Long Mynd.*

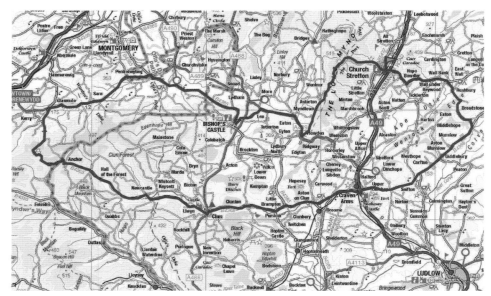

*Heading out to the border you will ride some sweet sections of road.*

The opening climb is relatively mellow and it's worth saving some energy for later as the final climb over the Long Mynd is very steep. You will pass through the picturesque village of Hope Bowdler, continuing east to Wall Under Heywood. Take a right turn and turn immediately left towards the village of Rushbury. The signage is slightly vague so take care and check your directions.

The route then passes the disused railway in Ape Dale before climbing up a short but steep climb through the trees on to Wenlock Edge. Once over the top a fast descent brings you down to the B4368 at Beambridge. Take it easy as the junction with the road below creeps up on you. Here take a right turn on to the B road heading in a south-westerly direction towards Craven Arms. You will cross back over the A49 taking a left at the mini-roundabout then turn right. Passing under the railway continue to head west on the B4368.

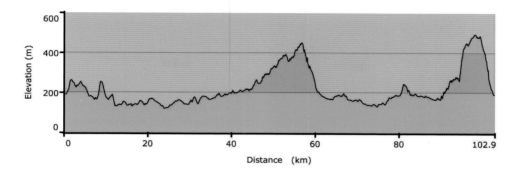

As you climb up through the village of Long Meadowend towards Aston on Clun you get some fantastic views of the rolling hillsides. The road continues west, running parallel with the River Clun and into the small town of its namesake. Cross over the A488 and continue heading west through more spectacular scenery.

Just beyond the village of Anchor you will pass over the border into Wales. Here on the most westerly tip of this route you will get some spectacular views into mid-Wales. As the road swings right there is a superb descent down through Block Wood. There are a few tight corners but visibility is relatively good. After a few kilometres you will come to a T-junction where you will turn right on to the A489. A relatively flat section of road leads you back towards Church Stoke into the Vale of Montgomery.

*Don't forget your passport!*

*The ruins of Clun Castle.*

This section is a welcome relief from the climbing and gives you a good chance to rest those legs before the final sting in the tail. A couple of kilometres before Church Stoke, take a right turn on to the B4385 heading towards Bishop's Castle. The route

*The descent is fast and rough in parts, the surface dressing is old and greasy in the trees.*

keeps to the edge of town but if you need some refreshments you can easily divert into the town centre.

Having dropped past the town centre join the main A488 and head north for a few hundred metres towards Lydham before bearing right on to the B4383. This section of road links you to the A489 where you should take a right turn and head east for approximately six kilometres. In the village of Plowden look out for a left turn that switches back on itself and is signposted towards Asterton. Just before this left turn is a large road sign indicating a road off to the right towards Lydbury North. The small country lane on your left is just a few hundred metres past this sign.

You will now be running alongside the western flank of the Long Mynd. This narrow road climbs steadily up towards the village of Asterton. As you enter the village look for a right turn climbing up over a cattle grid. The road then climbs up a very steep gradient hugging the hillside. If you get a chance take a look out to your left

where you have some spectacular views, however you may find due to the nature of the gradient that all you can see is your front wheel and asphalt!

As you crest of the hill, the road levels out and you get chance to ease the legs before the final but mellow rise climbs up across the top of the Long Mynd. As you traverse the hilltops, once again you have some absolutely stunning views. Hopefully they make the climb worthwhile.

*The views are stunning and the gradient leg burning.*

You will then start to make the final descent back into Church Stretton. The narrow road hugs the hillside as it winds its way back down towards the town. Some of the sections of asphalt are quite rough and there is a cattle grid just before you enter the treeline! A final blast down the treelined section of road brings you back into town at the end of the high street where you can pick up signs for the railway station.

# 20 CHURCH STRETTON 2: THE SHORT STING

**Start point:** Church Stretton railway station

**Grid ref:** SO 45529 93605

**Postcode:** SY6 6PG

**Total distance:** 68.4km

**Total elevation:** 1069m

**Max elevation:** 492m

## KEY CLIMBS

**From km 24 to km 41:** 146m climb over 17km

**From km 54 to km 59:** 96m climb over 5km

**From km 54 to km 63:** 329m climb over 9km

**Other key elevation gain:** From km 24 to km 63: elevation gain of 372m over 39km

**Exposure:** 4/5

The second loop is a shorter version of the larger Church Stretton loop. Head out in the same easterly direction through Ape Vale before climbing up on to Wenlock Edge and swinging round to the Craven Arms. The route then continues in a westerly direction towards Clun and then heads northwards to Bishop's Castle. From the picturesque town of Bishop's Castle, head back towards the east, crossing the Long Mynd. Once again you have some stunning sections of road passing through woodland, picturesque villages and historical sites.

Heading east over the main A49 trunk road pick up the B4371. Climb up through the avenue of trees and away from the town. In the village of Wall Under Heywood take a right turn then immediately left towards Rushbury. You will pass through Ape Dale before a short but stiff

*Beautiful borderland views.*

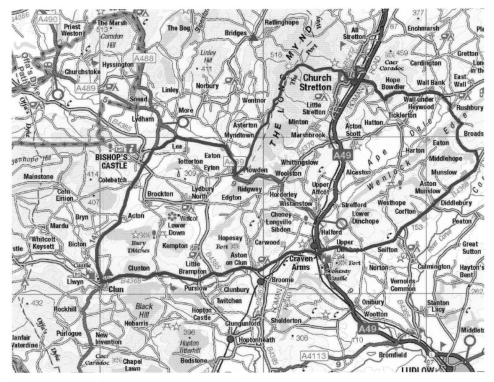

*The treelined climb up from Church Stretton.*

climb brings you up through the woodland on to Wenlock Edge. As you cross the hilltop you have some lovely views out across Corve Dale towards Brown Clee Hill and Titterstone Clee Hill, both easily recognisable with their radio masts proudly perched on top.

The route then swings westward on the B4360, backing towards Craven Arms. To the south of the town lies Stokesay Castle. This fortified manor house dates back to medieval times and has been lovingly preserved by English Heritage. It is considered one of the finest of its kind and is well worth a small diversion to go and take a look.

From the Craven Arms the route continues west, passing Aston on Clun and running parallel to the river up to the

*Clun Castle.*

village of Clun. This time take a right turn, passing the castle ruins on your left, and climb upwards towards Bishop's Castle. The road has lots of interest with good stiff climbs and stunning views.

The main road passes to the east side of Bishop's Castle. It's very easy to pop off the main route and take a look at the historical town centre. Just beyond Bishop's Castle, swing right on to the B4383 before joining the A489. After approximately six kilometres, look out for a left turn that switches back on itself and is signposted towards Asterton. Just before this left turn is a large road sign indicating a road off to the right towards Lydbury North. The small country lane on your left is just a few hundred metres past this sign.

The narrow road climbs up slightly towards the village of Asterton. As you enter the village take a right turn climbing up over the cattle grid on to the Long

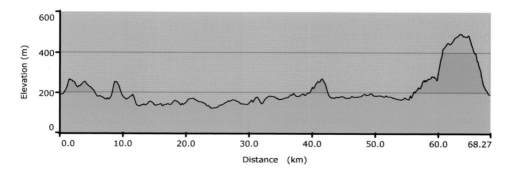

*Fast-rolling roads wind their way back towards Bishop's Castle.*

Mynd. A steep and narrow lane cuts up the hillside bringing you up on to the top of the Long Mynd. Follow the road across the hilltops where there are superb views of the surrounding area before you descend down the narrow steep hill back into Church Stretton. Take care down this descent as the surface is quite rough and you will pass over a cattle grid just before entering the treeline!

There are many blind corners and little room for passing oncoming traffic. Also note that the hilltops can become treacherous in wet and wintery conditions. The final treelined section brings you down into the town. At the crossroads head straight over picking up signs for the railway station on your right-hand side.

*The tough climb up on to the Long Mynd.*

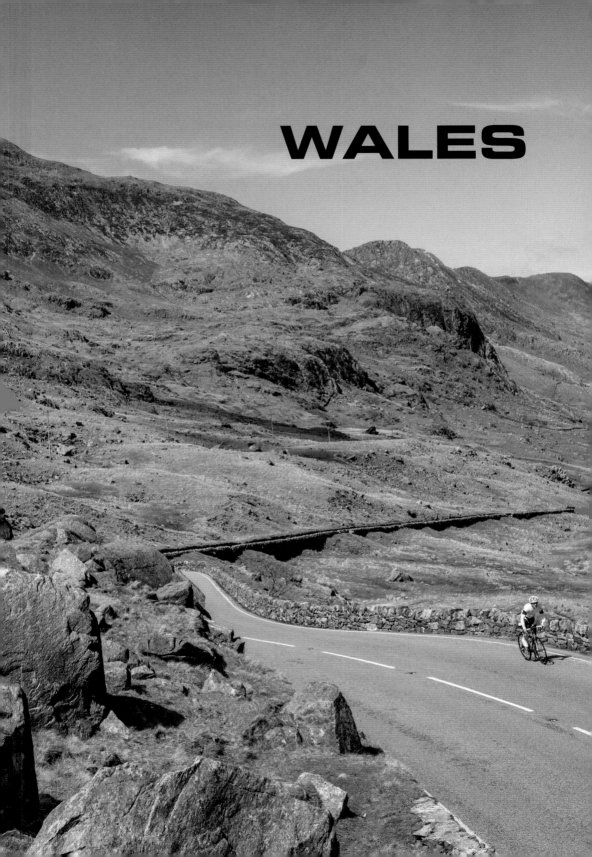

# WALES

# 21 LLANDOVERY: SEARCH FOR THE STIG

**Start point:** Llandovery railway station

**Grid ref:** SN 76376 34513

**Postcode:** SA20 0BG

**Total distance:** 86km

**Total elevation:** 1213m

**Max elevation:** 495m

## KEY CLIMBS

**From km 0 to km 16:** 192m climb over 16km

**From km 19.4 to km 31.7:** 195m climb over 12.3km

**From km 48 to km 62:** 417m climb over 14km

**Other key elevation gain:** From km 0 to km 31.7: elevation gain of 318m over 31.7km

**Exposure:** 4/5

*A fine reward for all the climbing.*

Located at the westerly end of the Black Mountains is the small town of Llandovery. This is the start point for a ride that will take you eastbound around the Glastfynydd Forest before turning southwards, climbing up past Cray Reservoir and heading over the Black Mountains. You will briefly enter the start of the Swansea Valley before climbing back up and over the Black Mountains through some spectacular scenery. The section of road that leads you northwards up over the mountains and back to Llandovery is frequently used by the motoring press – you may recognise the scenery from the BBC's popular motoring programme *Top Gear*. Expect to

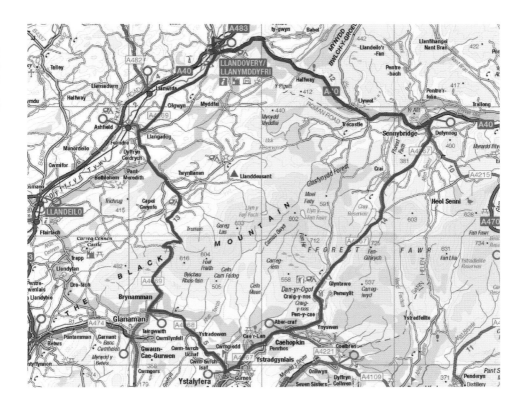

find some magnificent views, some tough challenging climbs and some high-speed descents with interesting sequences of corners throughout the loop.

Start by heading through Llandovery High Street towards Brecon. The opening section of this ride involves a lot of climbing, although the gradient on the trunk road is minimal and the surface good. The A40 is not a particularly busy trunk road but some sections are quite narrow. You should allow larger vehicles to pass where possible. Most of the time the road has ample width and good visibility.

When you reach the village of Sennybridge, take a turning to the right. Switching back to join the A4067, continue to climb upwards towards Cray Reservoir. As

you pass the reservoir and cross the pass you enter a fast downhill section. This provides a welcome relief to those legs having climbed for just over 30km from Llandovery.

*The long climb back up into the mountains starts with some steep gradients but the final few kilometres are more mellow.*

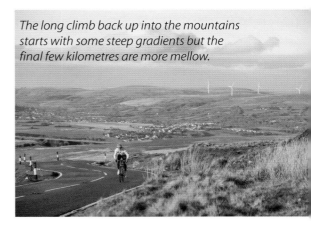

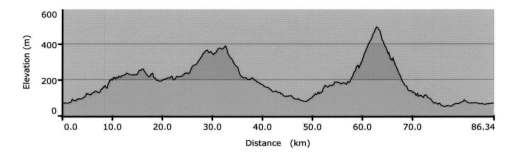

At the roundabout you will find a super-store should you wish to stop for some provisions before heading back up over the mountains.

The A4068 climbs uphill through several villages. There are a few steep gradients during this section and the general pattern is climbing. When you reach Brynamman look out for a right turn on to the A4069 which climbs up on to the hills towards Llangadog, The road snakes its way up the hillside offering spectacular views of the scenery around you. As you cross the hill a superb strip of asphalt lies before you in among the green rolling hillocks. As you descend, watch out for the wild horses and sheep that roam these hillsides.

*Super-smooth asphalt and fast-flowing corners.*

*The spectacular descent to Llangadog is often used by the motoring press for obvious reasons.*

The hillsides become steeper and the road twists its way through Glyntawe village past the country park. You will come to a roundabout where the route takes a right turn through the village of Gurnos.

Descend down the fast opening section into a tight right-hand switchback. The road continues to descend hugging the hillside – this really is a fantastic section of road. Further down the valley, you will pass through some picturesque woodland running next to the river and onwards and downwards to the village of Llangadog.

In the village take a right turn signposted towards Llandovery. The final few kilometres on the A4069 run parallel with the River Towy. The easy final section of road gives you a chance to warm down the legs before you finish back into Llandovery.

*Fast corners and amazing views.*

*The road back to Llangadog just keeps getting better and better the further down you get.*

# 22 BETWS-Y-COED 1: THE SNOWDON SNEAKY LAP

**Start point:** Betws-y-Coed railway station

**Grid ref:** SH 79534 56521

**Postcode:** LL24 0AE

**Total distance:** 82km

**Total elevation:** 1377m

**Max elevation:** 383m

## KEY CLIMBS

**From km 0 to km 17.5:** 363m of climb over 17.5km

**From km 61.2 to km 66:** 209m of climbing over 4.8km

**Other key elevation gain:** From km 61.2 to km 66: elevation gain of 206m over 4.8km

**Exposure:** 4/5

*The stunning Llanberis Pass.*

This spectacular loop takes you way out into the Snowdonia National Park and circumnavigates the Snowdon range. You'll cross Pen-y-Pass before dropping through Llanberis Pass into the town of Llanberis. Here lies the remains of Dolbadarn Castle, and the town is also the starting point for the Snowdonia mountain railway. The route then heads up towards Caernarfon where the spectacular castle sits high above the bay. The return leg brings you around the western side of Snowdon where, if you're lucky, you may get to see one of the steam trains running on the narrow gauge Welsh Highland railway. You will then climb back towards Capel Curig before descending past Swallow Falls back into Betws-y-Coed.

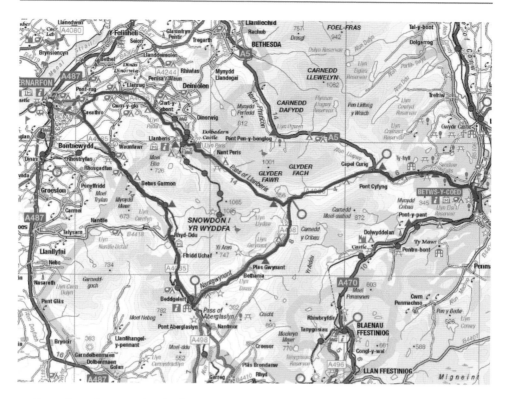

From the railway station in the centre of the town, head in a westerly direction along the A5. This old Roman road links London to the coastal town of Holyhead and is one of Britain's longest Roman roads. The climb levels out and you pass the Ugly House before climbing up again and on to Capel Curig. Take a left turn here, and you get your first views of the magnificent Snowdon range.

The A4086 climbs upwards towards the hotel and junction for Pen-y-Pass. At the junction are the remains of an old Roman camp. Take a right turn and climb up the pass. When you crest the hill the Llanberis Pass opens up in front of you, this spectacular valley is full of fascinating rock features. The fast descent means that you may not have time to take your eyes

*I don't think the Ugly house is all that ugly.*

off the road and absorb the spectacular nature of this valley.

The route then passes through the town of Llanberis where there are many

attractions. You will run alongside Llyn Padarn Lake, home to the Llanberis Lake Railway. Llanberis is also the start point for the mountain railway. The A4086 continues heading towards Caernarfon. Just outside the town the route takes a left turn just before the River Afon Seiont, the road is signposted towards Beddgelert and Porthmadog.

Pick up the A4085 heading in a south-easterly direction towards the small village of Beddgelert. This section of road is very picturesque with some stunning views of the surrounding hills. You will run alongside babbling brooks, picturesque lakes, through woodland and next to the Welsh Highland Railway.

LEFT: *The road out of Capel Curig and your first sighting of the Snowdon Range.*

BELOW: *Descending the Llanberis Pass between the drystone walls. The great surface means you can get a lick on.*

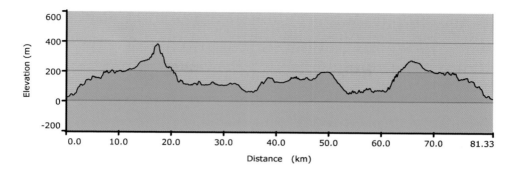

A fast descent past Beddgelert Forest will drop you into this pretty village. Here is a good chance to refuel before taking on the next pass. A long but steady climb winds its way up the valley back towards Capel Curig.

As you climb up out of the valley there are some stunning views of Snowdon over to your left. Here you rejoin your outward-bound route and simply retrace your steps back to the A5 descending down into Betws-y-Coed.

*The road back to Beddgelert gives you even more great views.*

# 23 BETWS-Y-COED 2: TAKE IT TO THE SLATE

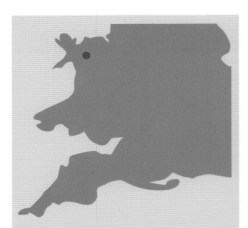

**Start point:** Betws-y-Coed station

**Grid ref:** SH 79534 56521

**Postcode:** LL24 0AE

**Total distance:** 70km

**Total elevation:** 1488m

**Max elevation:** 390m

## KEY CLIMBS

**From km 0 to km 16:** 255m of climb over 16km

**From km 37 to km 40:** 157m of climb over 3km

**From km 43 to km 54:** 379m of climb over 11km

**Exposure:** 3/5

*Superb Snowdon scenery.*

The second loop will take you out past Snowdon before hitting a fantastic fast-flowing decent into the village of Bedd-gelert. Past the village, the road continues to descend and some superb asphalt drops down through fast-flowing corners before you cross the river Afon Glaslyn and pick up more stunning roads leading to the Vale of Ffestiniog. Here a tough climb brings you up through the village of Blaenau

*The picturesque village splits up the long descent.*

Ffestiniog, famous for its large slate mines. You will then head over the Crimea Pass and follow the fast-rolling road down the valley back to Betws-y-Coed.

The opening leg from Betws-y-Coed is a carbon copy of the first ride. Follow the smooth fast-rolling A5 up to Capel Curig and swing left on to the A4086 and then the A498 towards Beddgelert. In the very fast downhill towards the village there are some tight corners but no real nasty surprises. Throughout this section you have beautiful views up into the horseshoe of the Snowdon range.

In the village of Beddgelert take a left turn over the stone bridge and follow the road out of the village before descending further down through some steep gradi-

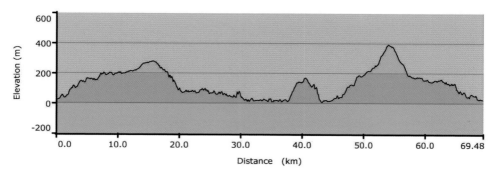

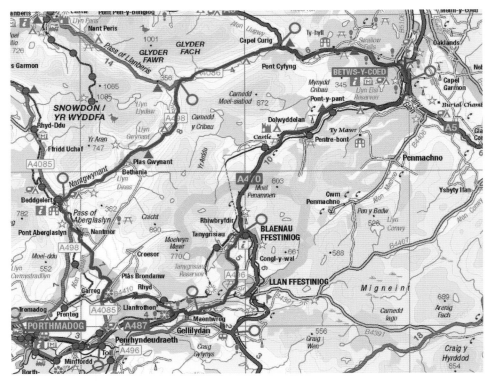

ents and fast corners. This really is a superb piece of road and is guaranteed to put a large smile on your face.

The descent last for a couple of kilometres before entering Pont Aberglaslyn where you will take a left turn over a stone bridge. The junction is just after a steep fast section and could be quite easily missed, so take care and keep your eye out for signs pointing to Penrhyndeudraeth and Dolgellau.

The following section of road twists its way up and down and is an absolute blast to ride, the surface is good and the

*Don't miss this left turn part way down the fast descent.*

*The tough climb up from Ffestiniog passes through the abandoned slate mines, the scene is really quite something.*

*The superb smooth long descent leads you back down the valley to Betws-y-Coed.*

views are stunning. In the village of Garreg look for the left turn on to the B4410. The road continues to twist and turn its way through the hillsides and there are some tough gradients to deal with. A fast down-hill section will bring you past the small lake of Llyn Mair beyond which a steep and fast section swings through along the left-hand corner and down to the main A487. The route swings left on to the main road. In several hundred metres takes a fork off left on to the A496. This road will lead you up the Vale of Ffestiniog.

You will now start the long climb up to-wards Blaenau Ffestiniog. When you arrive in the village, take a left turn on the main A470 signposted towards Betws-y-Coed. You will climb up some steep gradients as you pass through the old slate workings. The landscape here really does feel quite intimidating as the hillsides are strewn with the remains of years and years of mining the famous Welsh slate.

Having ridden over the Crimea Pass you start a long fast descent on good fast-rolling asphalt way back down the valley where you pick up the A5 hanging a left over the steel bridge back into Betws-y-Coed.

# THE NORTH, DERBYSHIRE DALES, YORKSHIRE DALES & PEAK DISTRICT

# 24 BUXTON: TRIP FOR A TART

**Start point:** Buxton railway station

**Grid ref:** SK 05922 73715

**Postcode:** SK17 6AQ

**Total distance:** 74km

**Total elevation:** 1273m

**Max elevation:** 400m

## KEY CLIMBS

**From km 20 to km 25:** 140m climb over 5km

**From km 46 to km 51.5:** 204m climb over 5.5km

**From km 55 to km 60:** 113m climb over 5km

**From km 65 to km 67:** 135m climb over 2km

**Exposure:** 3.5/5

*Lush green scenery and rolling hills.*

Buxton, the former Roman town of Aqvae Arnemetiae, is the gateway to the beautiful Peak District and start point for a fantastic loop that links to the town of Bakewell. This route takes in some stunning scenery and seriously fun sections of road as you head southwards from Buxton before cutting east through the edge of the Derbyshire Dales and on up to Bakewell. Rivers, woodland, quaint villages and rolling countryside: this ride has got the lot.

From the town centre pick up the A515 heading south. You will pass the hospital with the railway line to your left-hand side. The long straight section out of town crosses over the railway and this old Roman road climbs upwards towards Back

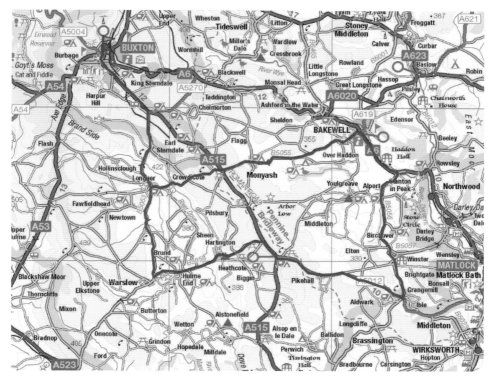

Dale and Brierlow Bar. Here, take a fork off to the right climbing up on to the B5053.

As you crest Hitter Hill you have some great views out to your right of the surrounding dales. The roads then descends through Glutton Bridge and on towards the village of Longnor. Continue straight through the village, passing over the River Manifold and on to Bridge End. Surrounded by lush green rolling hillsides the road continues in a southerly direction on the B5053 until you reach a junction on the left for the B5054.

A fast descent leads you down through Hulme End before climbing on up towards Hartington. The road snakes its way

*The picturesque landscape unfolds beyond the first climb.*

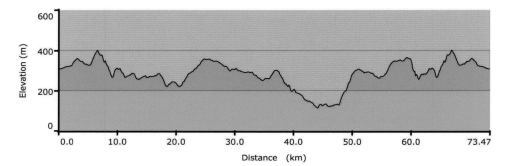

through the village and comes up to a T-junction with the main A515. Take care when pulling out on to the main road as you will have to take a right turn crossing the flow of traffic. Follow along for a few hundred metres before turning left in the village of Newhaven on to the quieter A5012.

Just outside the village you will pass over the Pennine bridleway and on to the long dale, a national nature reserve. The road continues in an easterly direction surrounded by lush rolling countryside to the village of Grangemill. Here take a left turn on the B5056 and head northwards towards Winster. The narrow B road winds its way along passing woodland, quaint

villages and fast-flowing rivers until it reaches the major trunk road, which leads you up into Bakewell.

You'll head northwards on the A6 passing Haddon Hall while running parallel to the River Wye. When you arrive in Bakewell pick up the B5055 heading west back towards Longnor. Shortly after the village of Monyash you will cross over the A515 trunk road. The road drops down a steep hill through Crowdicote village before entering Longnor. In the village centre you will come to a T-junction and should recognise this spot from earlier on your outward-bound section. Take a right turn and retrace your steps back up over the hills and on to Buxton.

*Just a short link on the A6 leads you to a Bakewell tart.*

# 25 LEEDS: TOUR DE FRANCE: LE TOUR 2014 GRAND DEPART (STAGE 1)

**Start point:** Leeds City Centre (railway station)

**Grid ref:** SE 29747 33364

**Postcode:** LS1 4DY

**End Point:** Harrogate City Centre (railway station)

**Grid ref:** 30397 55254

**Postcode:** HG1 1TE

**Total distance:** 206km (approximately)

**Total elevation:** 2595m (approximately)

**Max elevation:** 527m

## KEY CLIMBS

**From km 3 to km 8.5:** 126m climb over 5.5km

**From km 41 to km 48:** 144m climb over 7km

**From km 54 to km 87:** 307m climb over 33km

**From km 95 to km 118:** 364m climb over 23km

**From km 188 to km 206:** 105m climb over 18km

**Exposure:** 3/5

Having just celebrated its 100th anniversary in 2013, the Tour de France comes to Britain once again. Starting in the bustling city of Leeds, Stage 1 heads up through the Yorkshire Dales National Park, crossing the Pennines before dropping down into the city of Harrogate. The route takes in some stiff climbs and spectacular scenery while passing through picturesque villages along the way.

The long stages do however take in some major trunk roads, which is fine if you're cruising along in the pro peloton on closed roads but somewhat less appealing if you're heading out on your own. For this reason I have created two smaller loops

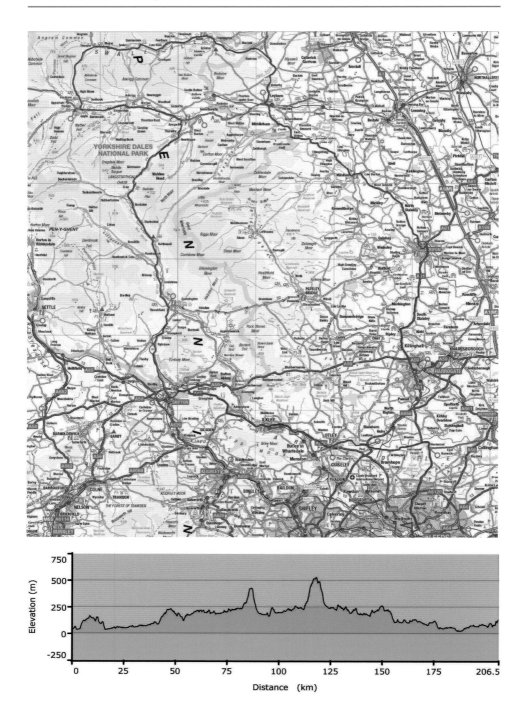

which take in some key climbs and quieter roads from the main stage.

The first stage of the tour departs Leeds. Heading north on the A61, the route cuts through the spectacular grounds of Harewood House, joining on to the A659 to Otley. From here the stage picks up the main A660, linking on to the A65 trunk road to Ilkley and on to Skipton. Heading north out of Skipton the stage joins some quieter roads as it climbs up around Embassy Moor on the B6265.

Heading north through Wharfedale the narrow road winds its way up the valley base into Bishopdale before a short but sharp climb from Thoralby links you to Wensleydale. The narrow road runs alongside the River Ure, heading west to Hawes. Another stiff climb links up and around Abbotside Common and Stags Fell into Swaledale, where the route heads east along the B6270 to Reeth and Grinton.

*The prize yellow jersey will be up for grabs once again as the Tour rolls out.*

The stage then swings round to the south, dropping down to Leyburn.

The going then gets somewhat easier as you head to Ripon where the route rejoins major trunk roads heading south to the finish in the city of Harrogate.

*Less French, fewer dusty vineyards, but the same peloton.*

# 26 LEYBURN: TASTE LE TOUR, PART 1

**Start point:** Leyburn railway station

**Grid ref:** SE 11698 90340

**Postcode:** DL8 5ET

**Total distance:** 113km

**Total elevation:** 1685m

**Max elevation:** 428m

## KEY CLIMBS

**From km 33 to km 45:** 218m climb over 12km

**From km 51.5 to km 57.5:** 285m climb over 16km

**From km 69 to km 89:** 244m climb over 20km

Starting from the small village of Leyburn, this edited loop starts off with some of the easiest sections heading south to Ripon.

*Team Sky's Bradley Wiggins hunts down Movistar's Nairo Quintana during the 2013 Tour of Britain.*

The smooth-flowing roads are a good way to get warmed up before heading out into the dales and taking on some of the more challenging roads from the 101st Le Tour. You will pass through some magnificent scenery as you head out into the Yorkshire Dales National Park.

From Leyburn head south on the A6108. These early kilometres are relatively easy as you head down to the village of Masham in the direction of Ripon. There are many picturesque villages on the route and you will skirt alongside crossing over the River Ure several times.

When you arrive in Ripon, the A road and Le Tour route take a hard left. Here you need to take a right turn and run down into the city centre on minor roads before heading out of the city centre in a westerly

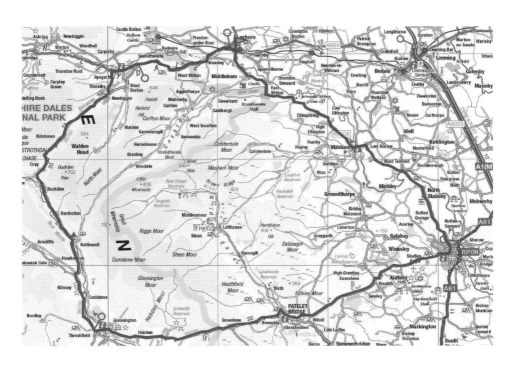

*Ripon city centre boasts some magnificent architecture.*

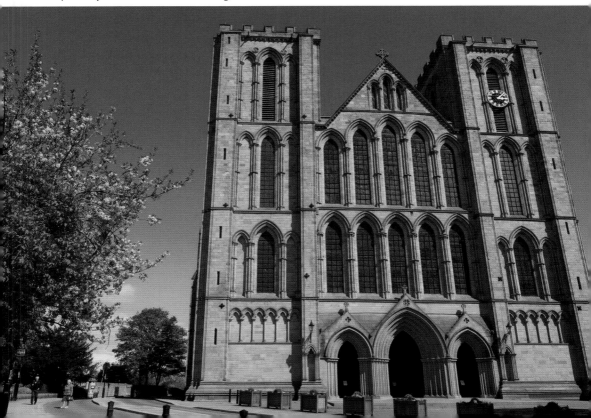

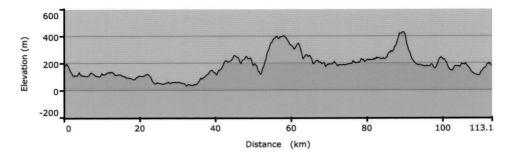

direction on the B6265 towards Pateley Bridge. Just outside the city you will pass Studley Park on your left-hand side and within a few kilometres a short but stiff climb brings you into the village of Risplith.

The road continues past Sawley Moor before you descend down into Pateley Bridge. Continue to follow the B road in a westerly direction, climbing up out of the steep gradient leading you up on to Bewerley Moor. Beyond the village of Greenhow you will start to descend across Craven Moor into Dibbles Bridge. Here the road drops down through the narrow bridge over the River Dibb before traversing the hills around to Hebden.

Beyond the village of Grassington, cross over the River Wharf and turn right on to the B6160 climbing up through Wharfedale, This spectacular section of road is covered in one of the previous routes and is worthy of a pro tour stage. From Wharfedale roll round into Bishopdale. The route then takes a left turn climbing on a minor road through the village of Thoralby into a steep climb up to Aysgarth. This is where the tour takes a left turn (you're more than welcome to add in this additional loop – Taste Le Tour, part 2 (see below) – for a longer ride) but this route takes a right turn, dropping down crossing the river linking back on to the A684 heading east back to the start point in Leyburn.

*The traffic may have lightened when you pass through.*

**Start point:** Leyburn railway station

**Grid ref:** SE 11698 90340

**Postcode:** DL8 5ET

**Total distance:** 70km

**Total elevation:** 1026m

**Max elevation:** 528m

## KEY CLIMBS

**From km 3 to km 33:** 420m climb over 30km

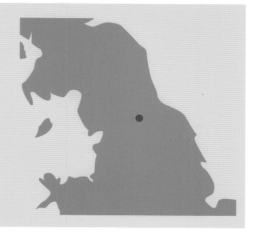

The second tour taster loop takes you from the village of Leyburn through Wensleydale and up into the spectacular scenery of the Pennines. You will make a lap around Abbotside Common and Stags Fell, linking into Swaledale and passing through spectacular scenery on superb roads.

From Leyburn, make a link via the A684 heading west to Aysgarth village along Wensleydale. Pick up Le Tour Stage

*Chris Froome in yellow on his way to Tour de France victory in 2013.*

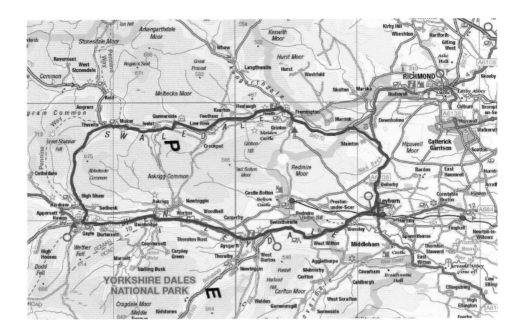

1 as you continue in a westerly direction along Wensleydale next to the River Ure. Spectacular scenery and quaint villages keep your mind busy as you climb up and drop down several times along the Dale heading to the village of Hawes.

In the village centre, take a right turn crossing the river heading north, climbing up past Hardraw Force around Abbotside Common and Stags Fell. You then link the downhill through the Butterstubs Pass and join the B6270 down into Muker. The road hugs the hillsides as you head along next to the river up through Swaledale to Reeth and Grinton. A few kilometres outside the village, bear right on to a minor road around Stainton Moor, heading south joining into the A6108 back to Leyburn.

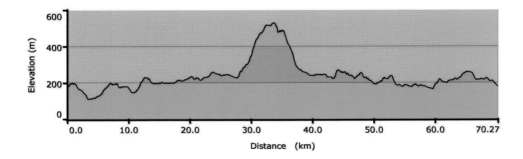

# 28 YORK: TOUR DE FRANCE: LE TOUR 2014 (STAGE 2)

**Start point:** York City Centre (railway station)

**Grid ref:** SE 59671 51698

**Postcode:** YO24 1AB

**End point:** Sheffield City Centre (railway station)

**Grid ref:** SK 35817 86779

**Postcode:** S1 2BP

**Total distance:** 208km (approximately)

**Total elevation:** 3633m (approximately)

**Max elevation:** 520m

## KEY CLIMBS

**From km 35 to km 52:** 230m climb over 17km

**From km 61.5 to km 65.5:** 140m climb over 4km

**From km 73 to km 85:** 345m climb over 12km

**From km 95 to km 105:** 292m climb over 10km

**From km 128 to km 144:** 448m climb over 16km

**From km 149 to km 156:** 192m climb over 7km

**Exposure:** 4/5

The second day of Le Tour 2014 starts in the historic city of York. The route heads out in a westerly direction towards Knaresborough, following the Roman road past Marston Moor, once again the route is using major trunk roads so we have provided a couple of alternative routes for you to savour the flavour of a pro tour stage.

From Knaresborough the route passes through Harrogate across Forest Moor and down towards Keighley. From here the tour stage cuts across the hilltops into Hebden Bridge along the Pennines before swinging round, passing through Huddersfield on its way to Sheffield. One last trip out into the hills takes the route from Holmfirth across Heyden Moor down to the Woodhead Reservoir. Here the stage picks up the main A628 trunk road heading east towards Stocksbridge

*The tour route passes through some stunning villages and British countryside.*

and on into the city of Sheffield.

The tour stage makes its way out of the city centre on the A19 before cutting across to the A59 heading west to Knaresborough. This section runs along the main trunk road and isn't particularly pleasant to ride – fast-moving traffic and impatient motorists make for sketchy going. The route crosses over the main A1(M) at a busy intersection before cutting through the picturesque town of Knaresborough and into Harrogate.

From Harrogate the tour route continues to head west up and over Blubberhouses Moor before descending down to the roundabout at Bolton Bridge. Here the stage picks up the B6160 down into Addingham before crossing the A65 joining the A6034 to Silsden. A section of

*Large trunk roads make up a fair amount of the tour route, so approach with caution or find an alternative route.*

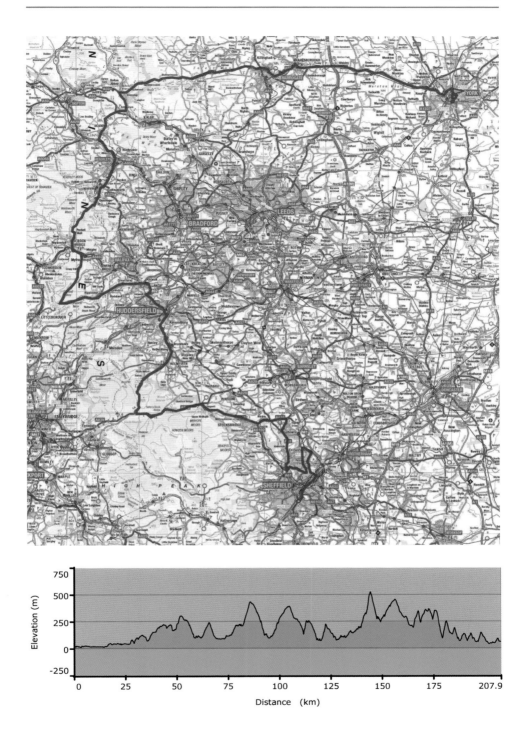

trunk road links the route into Keighley. Follow the A629 in a southerly direction before turning off on to the A6033 to Oxenhope.

This forms the start point for the two taster loops where the route climbs over Oxenhope Moor to Hebden Bridge. The main tour route then runs alongside the river on the A646 before turning right on to the B6138, heading south through Cragg Vale. The stage then heads east through Rippondene and follows the B6133 east to Elland before dropping south through Huddersfield, picking up the A6024 towards Holmfirth. From here the route climbs out on to the moorland crossing Heyden Moor before joining a fast downhill to the Woodhead Reservoir.

The riders will then take one final blast out into the hills as the stage takes them across Langsett Moors and on past Langsett Reservoir before joining minor roads around Broomhead Moor into the outskirts of Sheffield. The stage finishes in Sheffield city centre before the riders load up and head south to Cambridge for Stage 3.

*Milestone marker just outside Oxenhope.*

# 29 OXENHOPE: TASTE LE TOUR, PART 3

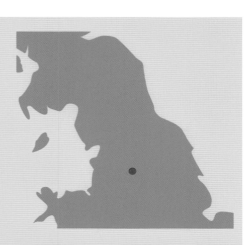

**Start point:** Oxenhope railway station

**Grid ref:** SE 03223 35317

**Postcode:** HX7 6JE

**Alternative start point:** Hebden Bridge railway station

**Grid ref:** SD 99436 26920

**Postcode:** HX7 6JE

**Total distance:** 56.5km

**Total elevation:** 1258m

**Max elevation:** 432m

## KEY CLIMBS

**From km 0 to km 4:** 228m climb over 4km

**From km 11 to km 18:** 322m climb over 7km

**From km 30 to km 35:** 145m climb over 5km

**From km 42.5 to km 46.5:** 180m climb over 4km

**Exposure:** 4/5

*A short but stiff climb heads out of Oxenhope.*

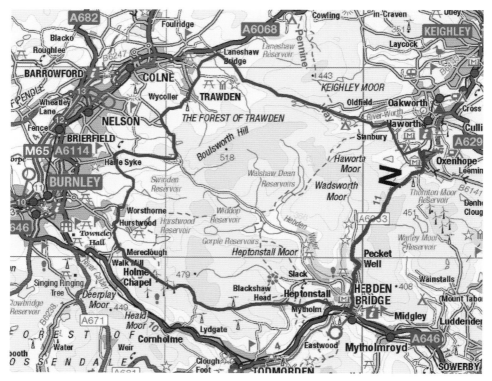

We've put together two rides that take in a key section of the second stage from York to Sheffield. The link from Oxenhope over Cock Hill to Hebden Bridge may be a short one but it is a sweet one. The surrounding lanes give you the chance to complete a ride in stunning scenery avoiding major roads.

*Open rugged hilltops are exposed and can be arduous on a windy day.*

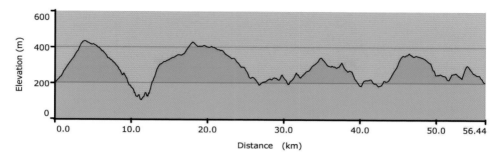

The sweet little climb up out of Oxenhope brings you up between drystone walls into the open ground of Oxenhope Moor. The road then snakes its way down the valley's side into Hebden Bridge, where the main tour route heads off on the major trunk road. The first of two loops heads west climbing up a steep narrow lane out of the town on to Stansfield Moor. Here the route passes through some spectacular scenery, crossing the Limestone Trail on to the village of Mereclough. The route then heads northwards on the narrow lanes to Cockden on to Trawden before swinging round to the east following the Brontë Way back towards Oxenhope.

*Climbing is dirty work for Joaquim Rodríguez of Team Katusha.*

# 30 OXENHOPE: TASTE LE TOUR, PART 4

**Start point:** Oxenhope railway station

**Grid ref:** SE 03223 35317

**Postcode:** BD22 9LB

**Alternative start point:** Hebden Bridge railway station

**Grid ref:** SD 99436 26920

**Postcode:** HX7 6JE

**Total distance:** 30 km

**Total elevation:** 763m

**Max elevation:** 434m

## KEY CLIMBS

**From km 0 to km 4:** 226m climb over 4km

**From km 10.5 to km 12.5:** 185m climb over 2km

**From km 17.5 to km 24.5:** 273m climb over 7km

**Exposure:** 4/5

*Yorkshire has a beauty of its own.*

Once again, take the sweet little climb out of Oxenhope up and over Cock Hill. Following the stage of Le Tour 2014, drop down into Hebden Bridge. This edited route then follows minor roads east, hugging Crow Hill Nook before climbing up to Wainstalls village on the narrow lanes. From here the route climbs high up into the hills along Cold Edge before passing over Warley Moor and Warley Reservoir. From the high hilltops you have some spectacular views of the surrounding landscape as you pass the wind farm before descending through Oxenhope Moor back into the town. There is a section of rough, poorly surfaced road

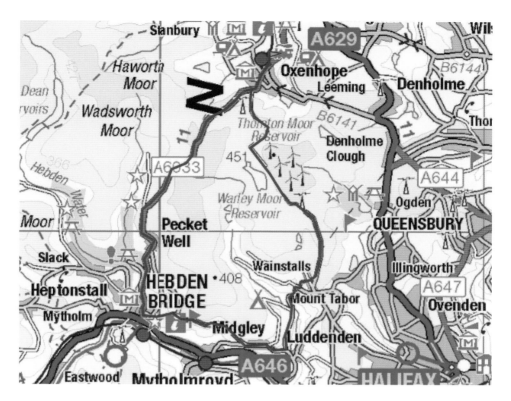

that lasts for several hundred metres up by the wind farm so please take this into consideration when selecting your tyres and wheels.

Ascending this key climb from the village centre, head in a southerly direction up on to Cock Hill passing Keeper's Lodge. Over the summit a fast descent drops you down through Pecket Well into Hebden Bridge. Just before the main road pick up a narrow country lane on your left and start a steep climb round the hillside to Midgley village. The narrow lane drops down a steep gradient to the edge of Luddenden village where you will take a left turn climbing up to the village of Booth, the road forks right and drops down over the river before climbing up another steep

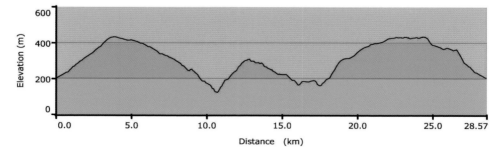

*Every racer's dream, a stage win.*

gradient passing the village of Wainstalls up on to Cold Edge.

The road then climbs up across Warley Moor where you will see the wind farm in the distance. This is where you will encounter that poor surface. The road then descends down a steep gradient through a tight right-hand corner as you cross

Oxenhope Moor. Take care further down the hill and you will pass over a cattle grid before dropping down another steep gradient past the small chapel back to the main A6033. Here you take a right turn and descend back down to the village where you started the loop.

# 31 SETTLE 1: LITTONDALE LOOP

**Start point:** Settle railway station

**Grid ref:** SD 81654 63454

**Postcode:** BD24 9AA

**Total distance:** 64km

**Total elevation:** 1063m

**Max elevation:** 432m

## KEY CLIMBS

**From km 0 to km 6.5:** 423m of climbing over 6.5km

**From km 9 to km 13:** 122m climb over 4km

**From km 48 to km 59:** 278m climb over 11km

**Exposure:** 4/5

*Wide open roads and big country.*

The first of two loops is a shorter option to give you a chance to savour the delights of the larger loop which heads out way into the Yorkshire Dales National Park. Expect some stunning views on both of the Settle loops as majestic ribbons of asphalt snake along between drystone walls. This shorter loop takes you around several high peaks on quiet roads leading to and along Littondale where you will run parallel to the River Skirfare.

From the town centre head north on the B6479, running parallel to and crossing over the railway. In just over a kilometre take a right turn in the village of Langcliffe where you will climb up the steep narrow lane. The road continues to climb through the patchwork quilt of lush green fields broken up by drystone walls and grey

rocky outcrops. There is little shelter and I don't recommend riding these routes in poor weather conditions.

Crest the hill and continue to follow a narrow strip of asphalt across the hilltops. Over in the distance you can see the prominent peak of Pen-y-ghent. You will come to a T-junction where the route takes a left turn. Take care on the steep descent as you pass over a cattle grid before rising back up to a farm on your right. At the T-junction take a right, continuing to follow the narrow lane heading out into the dales

The road continues to climb up between drystone walls to Dawson Close. Finally, you leave the walls behind and make your descent down to Halton Gill. There are a few cattle grids throughout this section of road but they are all clearly

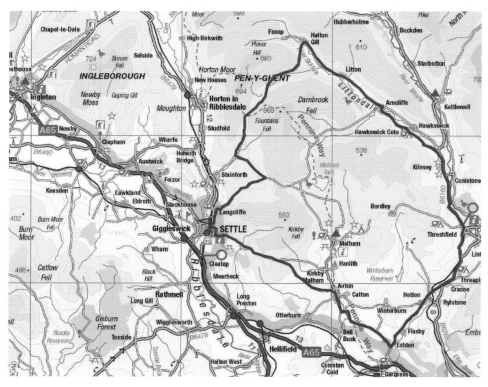

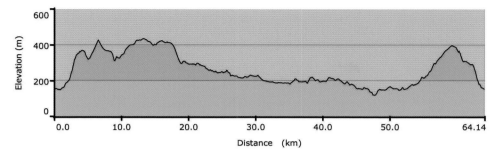

Elevation (m)

Distance (km)

marked. At Halton Gill take a right turn and start to head south-east along Littondale, passing through the village of Arncliffe below Hawkswick Clowder.

The road then joins into the B6160 and along Wharfedale as you head south towards Grassington. You won't quite make it into Grassington as you pick up a right turn on to the B6256 at Threshfield village. Throughout this route you're surrounded by stunning scenery, the rocky outcrops have a model railway-like feel to them and the vastness of the landscape is very humbling.

Just beyond the village of Cracoe look for a right-hand fork signposted towards Hetton. The minor road passes through Hetton and on to Flasby before taking a turning on the right, heading up through

Eshton village. This section of road leads to Airton village where you take a left turn in the village centre heading out across Scosthrop Moor. The rolling hills and high hedges hide the road at times so take care as there is not a huge amount of room to pass oncoming vehicles.

The road continues in a north-westerly direction back towards Settle. Before Settle you will pass over a small stream that feeds Scaleber Force – the waterfall is not visible from the road but it is certainly audible. A fast downhill between drystone walls feeds you back down towards the town. There are some tight corners so take care particularly if the road is wet. Follow the road into the centre of town where you can easily navigate your way back to the railway station.

*Britain in bloom.*

# 32 SETTLE 2: DALE DELIGHT

**Start point:** Settle railway station

**Grid ref:** SD 81654 63454

**Postcode:** BD24 9AA

**Total distance:** 110km

**Total elevation:** 1524m

**Max elevation:** 438m

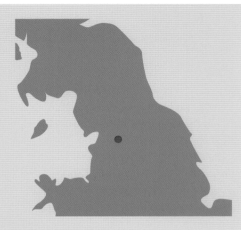

## KEY CLIMBS

**From km 0 to km 26:** 286m climb over 26km

**From km 52 to km 62:** 277m climb over 10km

**From km 92 to km 104:** 278m climb over 12km

**Exposure:** 4/5

*Climbing through the moorland.*

The second Settle loop is a real classic. It has a perfect blend of easy climbs, tough climbs, fast descents and of course stunning scenery. Head northwards through Horton Moor past Simon Fell around the high peak of Ingleborough at 724m on up into the Yorkshire Dales National Park and along the famous Wensleydale. Return through the National Park, crossing Langstrothdale Chase and along Wharfedale before joining into a shorter loop near the village of Kilnsey.

From Settle, head northwards on the B6479. Alongside the railway, you will pass through Horton in Ribblesdale surrounded by rolling hills and rocky outcrops. The route also follows the river Ribble as you climb up towards Ribblehead. Take a right turn here, picking up the B6255 and

*Smooth roads wind their way around the hills. It's hard graft in the wind but the rewarding views make it worthwhile.*

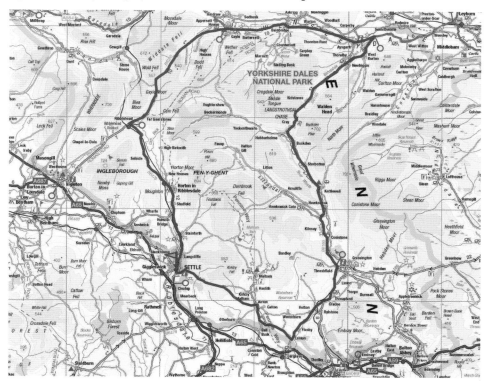

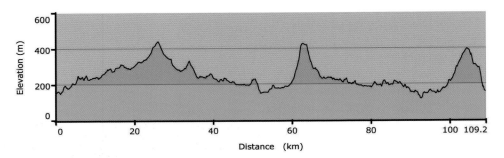

climbing up towards Gayle Moor. The road joins into Widdale below Widdale Fell and swings round to the east into the village of Hawes.

From here, join into Wensleydale, passing through Bainbridge running alongside the River Ure to Aysgarth. At this quaint little village start to head southwards, joining on to the B6160 and along Bishopdale. A stiff climb leads up out of Bishopdale before you descend down to the River Wharfedale and the village of Buckden. Le Tour 2014 heads along this route in the opposite direction.

The route follows Wharfedale, heading in a southerly direction picking up loop 1 near the village of Kilnsey. As per the shorter loop, head down towards Grassington and take a right turn on to the B6265 through Threshfield. Continue along the B road and take the right fork just beyond the village of Cracoe heading towards and signposted to Hetton.

From Hetton, continue in a south-westerly direction before taking a right turn up through the village of Eshton, from Eshton the narrow lane heads north-west to Airton. In the village you need to take the second left just before the village green and head up crossing Scosthrop Moor. The rolling narrow lane brings you back in to Settle via a fast descent.

*Descending down into Hawes.*

# THE NORTH-WEST, LAKE DISTRICT

# 33 WINDERMERE 1: THE 30%

**Start point:** Windermere railway station

**Grid ref:** SD 41426 98704

**Postcode:** LA23 1AH

**Total distance:** 84km

**Total elevation:** 1927m

**Max elevation:** 418m

## KEY CLIMBS

**From km 11 to km 14:** 110m climb over 3km

**From km 34 to km 36:** 103m climb over 2km

**From km 38 to km 45:** 203m climb over 7km

**From km 50 to km 59:** 393m climb over 9km

**From km 61 to km 64.5:** 173m climb over 4.5km

**Exposure:** 4.5/5

*Sunset and stiff climbs in the Lakes.*

This classic Lakeland ride takes you up and over two iconic passes. Anybody who has ridden the Fred Whitton challenge will be familiar with both Hardnott and Wynross passes. These two passes form a section of the much longer route used on the Fred Whitton challenge. The challenge is an annual charity ride that takes in some of the toughest climbs in the Lakes. Fred was the racing secretary of the Lakes Road Club, sadly passing away in 1998 age 50, and the ride was created in his memory.

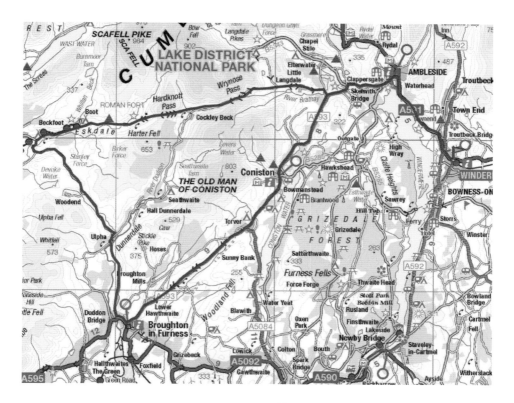

Expect some very stiff climbs with steep gradients and narrow twisty Lakeland roads. Some of the hilltops are rather exposed and it is not advisable to ride these routes in adverse weather, however, on a clear day the views are spectacular and scenery truly breathtaking. Although this is the shorter of the two Windermere routes it does have the most amount of climbing, an indicator of the steep gradients that await you.

Starting from Windermere, head northwards on the main A591 to the picturesque town of Ambleside. In Ambleside, pick up the one-way system and head out of town in a westerly direction towards

*Undulating, narrow, steep spectacular roads in the heart of the Lake District.*

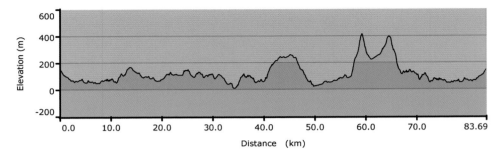

Skelwith Bridge on the A593. The initial section of road undulates and snakes its way along next to the River Brathay. Beyond Skelwith Bridge the road climbs upwards and around Park Fell, heading towards Coniston. The road drops down passing through High and Low Yewdale before coming into the quaint village of Coniston.

Passing Coniston Water, where Donald Campbell broke several speed records in his craft Bluebird, the route continues

*Open roads allow you to enjoy the descents – the surface is lumpy and quite harsh at times.*

heading south-westerly to the small town of Broughton in Furness. The rolling road has a few steep gradients, and it's worth conserving a little energy for the climbs on the passes ahead as you ride this section of road.

In Broughton in Furness, take a right turn on to the A595. In approximately one kilometre at Duddon Bridge the route takes a right on to a minor road heading north. You're presented with your first stiff climb as you head up towards Whistling Green. In the village, take a right turn. Just over the bridge and within a few hundred metres a left turn at Ulpha links into another steep uphill section. The road continues to climb up through Crosbythwaite and on to Birker Fell.

Here a fast downhill section brings you down towards Eskdale Green. Just before the village, take the right turn. The road makes its way steadily up the valley towards Hardknott Pass. The pass climbs up with some steep gradients and tight switchbacks. Then the road levels out for a short section before climbing up past the remains of a Roman fort and into more tough switchbacks and a steep gradient. Once you've crossed the pass the descent is no picnic either – the asphalt surface has become like a washboard from cars struggling to find traction on the steep inclines.

*The long descent from Wynross Pass.*

*Tight switchbacks in both the climbs and descents.*

The tight corners mean that speed is to be kept well under control as you descend down into Wynross Bottom.

As you ride along the valley base you can see the narrow tarmac lane climbing up the pass ahead. You will once again encounter some steep gradients and tight corners as you ascend Wynross Pass. Once over the pass the rough descent brings you down to the village of Little Langdale. A few more kilometres of undulating asphalt links you back on to the A593.

From here simply retrace your steps back through Skelwith Bridge and on to Ambleside. From Ambleside it is just a few kilometres back down the A591 to Windermere.

# 34 WINDERMERE 2: TEBAY TESTER

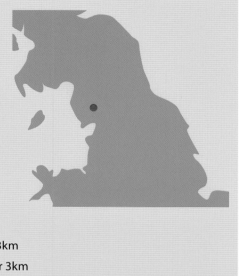

**Start point:** Windermere railway station

**Grid ref:** SD 41426 98704

**Postcode:** LA23 1AH

**Total distance:** 104km

**Total elevation:** 1568m

**Max elevation:** 456m

## KEY CLIMBS

**From km 0 to km 11:** 313m climb over 11km

**From km 41 to km 59:** 201m climb over 18km

**From km 74 to km 77:** 131m climb over 3km

**From km 89 to km 102:** 136m climb over 3km

**Exposure:** 4/5

*The Kirkstone Pass.*

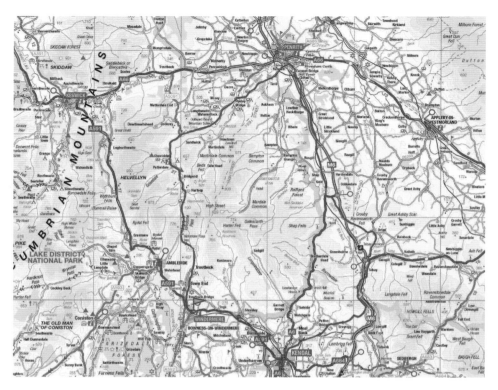

The second and longer loop from Windermere covers just over 100 kilometres
and over 1500m of climbing and takes in
another classic pass from the Fred Whitton
challenge. The route snakes alongside
Ullswater on a magnificent stretch of
asphalt before heading out of the national
park towards Penrith. From here the
route heads southwards, cutting its way
through the countryside, crossing the M6
motorway and on to the larger town of
Kendle. Once again there are magnificent
views and spectacular sections of road.
High passes and ample climbing rewarded
by some superb descents.

*The road winds its way up the hill from
Windermere between drystone walls.*

From the railway station in Windermere head along the main A591 before picking up a right turn on to the A592 towards the Kirkstone Pass. The climb winds its way up the valley, hugging the hillsides and snaking along between rocky outcrops and drystone walls. You will cross over Trout Beck and head up through open ground, cresting the hill past the public house on your right-hand side. A fast

*The top of the Kirkstone Pass and a chance for some refreshments.*

descent with good surface leads down from the pass before levelling out past Brothers Water and on to Patterdale at the foot of Ullswater.

The road makes its way up around Ullswater, climbing up and dipping down on super-smooth asphalt. This fast-rolling section really is a lot of fun but do take into consideration there is still plenty more climbing to do and some fair distance to cover.

Leave Ullswater behind at Pooley Bridge and join the B5320 heading north-east towards Penrith. You will pass over the motorway and come to a T-junction in Eamont Bridge. Just to the north of here lies the historic town of Penrith. This is also the start point for other routes contained within this book. Should you wish to do so you can pick up another loop from Penrith, making for a much longer (and tougher) ride. This route, however, takes a right and follows the A6 heading towards Shap.

You will cross over the M6 motorway a few times and pass through Shap village. On the far side of the village you pass a stone circle. There are many of these in the area, so keep an eye out in the fields surrounding you as you pass through the lush rolling countryside. Take a left turn towards the motorway and then a right turn on to the B6261.

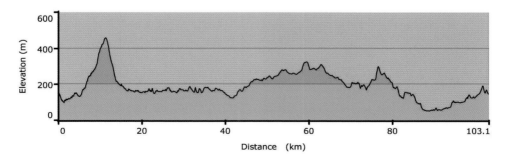

*Ullswater and some fine undulating smooth asphalt around the lakeside.*

The road winds its way through open farmland passing underneath the motorway down to the village of Orton. From here continue to descend down to Tebay. Passing through the village, pick up the

*Heading down to Tebay having passed Shap summit.*

A685, climbing up over the motorway and around the hillside. The following kilometres dip down and climb up several times as you head towards Kendal. In the town are the remains of an old castle and all the usual amenities of modern-day Britain.

Having navigated your way through the town centre crossing the railway and river, pick up the A528 towards Windermere for a short distance before turning right towards Burneside. Basically, you will head back in the direction of Windermere, trying your best to avoid using the main trunk road. There are a multitude of small lanes you can pick up to avoid using the trunk road. The route continues passing through Staveley where you then join the A591 for the final few kilometres back into Windermere.

# 35 KESWICK: BUTTERMERE BLAST

**Start point:** Keswick town centre

**Grid ref:** NY 26697 23526

**Postcode:** CA12 5JD

**Total distance:** 45km

**Total elevation:** 1017m

**Max elevation:** 368m

## KEY CLIMBS

**From km 0 to km 7.7:** 275m climb over 6km

**From km 26.5 to km 30:** 252m climb over 3.5km

**Other key elevation gain:** From km 14 to km 30: elevation gain of 292m over 16km

**Exposure:** 4/5

In this Lakeland classic you will take on a lap of the Derwent Fells, the route heads out climbing up through Whinlatter Forest and round Grasmoor peak then back through Buttermere Fell before crossing the Honister Pass, descending through Borrowdale and along the eastern flank of Derwent Water. This short sub-50-kilometre loop takes in more spectacular Lakeland scenery and covers just over 1000 metres of climbing. Once again you're faced with steep gradients and interesting winding Lakeland roads.

Leave Keswick town centre and head along the B5289, joining the main A66 to Braithwaite village. From here, pick up the minor road twisting through the village and climbing up the stiff gradients

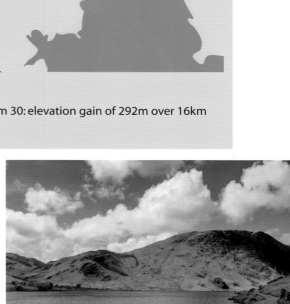

*Buttermere in all its glory.*

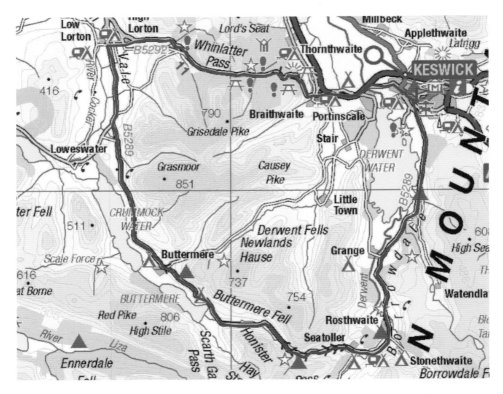

heading towards Whinlatter Forest. You get a wonderful view as you pass the car park on your right looking out towards Skiddaw. This is a busy section of road as the forest above Braithwaite is popular with tourists, so be sure to take care through the narrow village before you start your climb.

Follow the B5292 through the forest and along the Whinlatter Pass before descending into High Lorton where you will take a left turn down to Low Lorton. The route now runs southwards along Lorton Vale and you get a chance to rest the legs before taking the fork left at Brackenthwaite towards Crummock Water and Buttermere. The road undulates as it follows the lakeside into Buttermere village. A short sharp gradient leads you

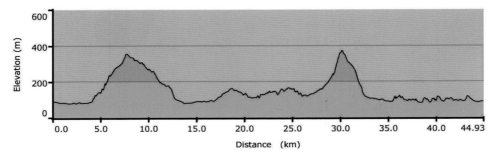

*The first pass climbs up through Whinlatter Forest.*

out of the village and alongside the banks of Buttermere Water.

Steep hillsides and rocky escarpments surround you as you ride through this picture-postcard landscape before the climb up the Honister Pass. The pass starts with some easier gradients and steepens up in the latter stages. Up on top of the pass you will see the slate-mining museum and cafe to your left. On a clear day the

*A classic Lakeland scene, narrow undulating roads and rocky hillsides.*

*The climb up the Honister Pass gets steeper near the top.*

views from either side are breathtaking. You will now drop down towards Rosthwaite village. The descent is rough in places with some steep gradient and you will also pass over a cattle grid!

The remaining kilometres wind their way back towards Keswick along the valley of Borrowdale to Derwent Water. This section of road can get quite busy throughout the holiday season as it is a popular spot with tourists. Take care on the twisty roads and savour the views across Derwent Water before you're back in the bustling Lakeland town of Keswick.

# THE NORTH, PENNINES

# 36 PENRITH 1: BRAMPTON BASH

**Start point:** Penrith railway station

**Grid ref:** NY 51213 29894

**Postcode:** CA11 7JQ

**Total distance:** 98km

**Total elevation:** 1217m

**Max elevation:** 574m

## KEY CLIMBS

**From km 0.5 to km 3:** 112m climb over 2.5km

**From km 13.5 to km 21:** 147m climb over 7.5km

**From km 57 to km 75:** 375m climb over 18km

**Other key elevation gain:** From km 13.5 to km 75: elevation gain of 501m over 61.5 km

**Exposure:** 4/5

*The first crossing of the River Eden just past Lazonby.*

The small but busy town of Penrith lies neatly between the Lake District and the Pennines. Out to the east of the town in the northern tip of the Pennines you will find some fantastic riding. Quiet roads take you way out into this grand landscape where there are many small villages and hidden gems to discover.

The first ride from Penrith is a shorter loop which takes you north, skirting along the edge of the hills towards the town of Brampton before heading south to the quaint village of Alston. From here climb up and over Gamblesby Fell past the Hartside Cafe before descending back down into Penrith.

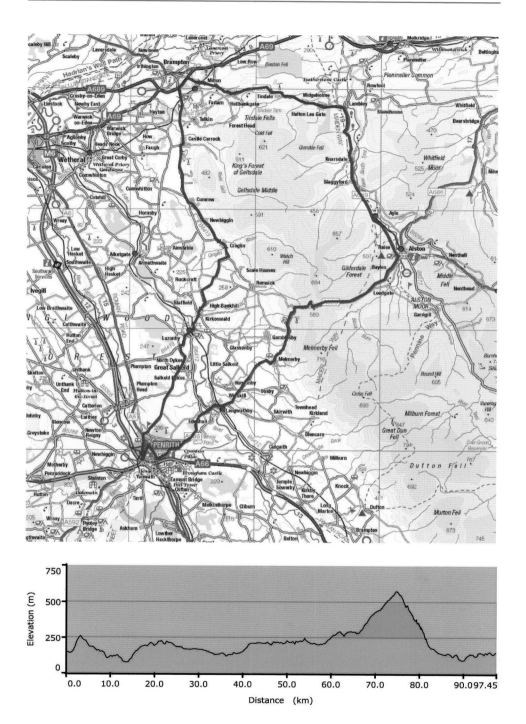

*Sandstone buildings and stone walls, the opening half of the ride is easy-going but the tough work lies ahead.*

From the railway station, skirt around the eastern side of the town centre, picking up the A6 heading north. Just before leaving the town, bear right and climb up past the golf course on Beacon Hill towards the village of Lazonby. Look out for a right turn at a crossroads and drop down to the village of Great Salkeld. As you descend into the village bear round to the left on to the B6142.

In Lazonby the route takes a right turn at the T-junction, passing underneath the railway before crossing the Eden River. Continue to follow the road in a northerly direction up through the village of Castle Carrock and on past the Talking Tarn. You will cross over the railway line. Just beyond the signs for the Talking Tarn you need to take a right turn into a minor road towards Brampton station. Follow the narrow lane past Brampton station to a T-junction where you take a left turn over the railway and roll on for several hundred metres before joining the A689 in Milton.

*Rolling roads and great views in the distance of the central Lakes.*

The route now takes a right turn on the main road passing around the northern tip of Bruthwaite Forest and Tindale Fell.

Swing around the south side of Hartleyburn Common before bearing right and heading deep into the hills in a southward direction. The road hugs the hillsides, making its way along the valley dropping down through Slaggyford passing Snope Common over to the left and Knarsdale Common to your right. These large rolling hillsides almost hide their summits and scale. Then you will ride alongside the river South Tyne to down to Alston.

Just outside the village, follow the signs and join the main A686 back towards Penrith. Passing along the southern edge of Gilderdale Forest the road starts to climb up to the Hartside café. The views on the top here are truly spectacular as you look across towards the Lake District in the distance. The descent down from the cafe is an absolute blast too – there are some fantastic sequences of corners and the road is wide enough that you can carry some good speed as you snake your way down the hillside.

The final section of road back to Penrith does undulate slightly but the majority of the hard work is done now. Before you reach the main A66 take a right turn into the town centre back to the railway station.

*Great views down the valley as you drop down towards Alston.*

# 37 PENRITH 2: THE PENRITH PENNINE PUNISHER

**Start point:** Penrith railway station

**Grid ref:** NY 51213 29894

**Postcode:** CA11 7JQ

**Alternative start point:** Langwathby railway station

**Grid ref:** NY 57321 33444

**Postcode:** CA10 1NZ

**Total distance:** 154km

**Total elevation:** 2559m

**Max elevation:** 625m

## KEY CLIMBS

**From km 9.5 to km 25:** 483m climb over 15.5km

**From km 33.5 to km 44:** 348m climb over 10.5km

**From km 67 to km 70:** 182m climb over 3km

**From km 72 to km 76:** 210m climb over 4km

**From km 86.5 to km 110:** 380m climb over 23.5km

**From km 122.5 to km 131:** 295m climb over 8.5km

**Exposure:** 4.5/5

The second ride out into the North Pennines from Penrith provides a real challenge, but the sweet reward of fantastic scenery and amazing roads should be enough to entice you out into the wild landscape. Head up past the Hartside Cafe and descend down past Gilderdale Forest and into the village of Alston. The route heads deep into the Pennines on to Weardale and down to Middleton in Teesdale. Here you can stop and refuel before making the climb back up through Teesdale over Langdon Beck towards Alston. You now retrace your steps climbing up past the Hartside Cafe once more before the final blast back into Penrith.

With well over 2000 metres of climbing and a snippet over 150 kilometres this route is not for the faint-hearted: long climbs, exposed hilltops and fast descents are the order of the day on this truly epic and spectacular ride.

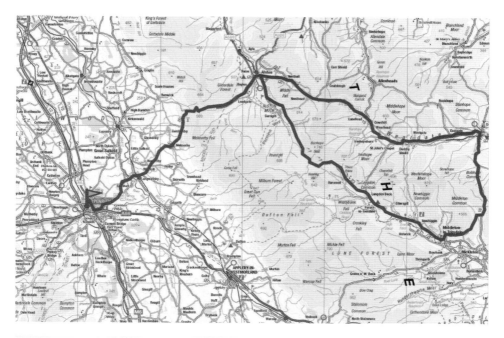

*The downhill into Alston.*

From Penrith town centre, head out east, picking up the A686 and crossing over the River Eden through the village of Langwathby. In another few kilometres, pass through Melmerby where you will start to climb up towards Gamblesby Fell and the Hartside Cafe. The gradients in the climb are relatively mellow and the road has lots of interest as it twists around the hill offering spectacular views back across to the Lake District.

A long mellow downhill brings you into the pretty village of Alston where you will take the right turn in the village centre, climbing up on the rough cobbles before forking left on to the A689. This tough little climb brings you around the north side of Alston Moor and Middle Fell. You will pass the heritage centre at Nenthead and a superb downhill leads down into the valley past Killhope Lead Mining Centre.

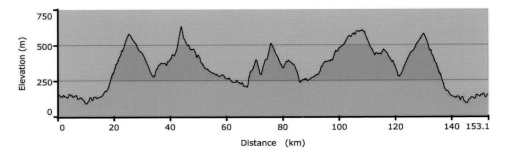

From here the road swings back on itself and after a few hundred metres crosses the river and swings back on itself again. Just beyond the railway crossing climb up a steep hill through some switchbacks up on to Catterick Moss. Here you can see the road on the far side of the valley snaking across the open moorland. The scale of the scenery is just phenomenal – many people are unaware that the British Isles has such vast open areas of land. The road then descends down and climbs up on to Bollihope Common.

*A rare section of cobbles as you climb up through Alston village.*

The road drops down through Cowshill village and on to Wearhead. The hillsides are strewn with drystone walls and abandoned stone buildings, remnants of a bygone era of mining throughout this region. Following the River Wear, run along Weardale to the town of Stanhope. As you descend down into the town be careful not to miss a right turn for the B6278 towards Middleton in Teesdale.

*The open hilltops give you a great view of the road ahead. The road dips in and out of large valleys so expect some tough climbs.*

Keep your eye out for a sign indicating to Alston, High Force and Middleton in Teesdale to your right. Take this road on the right switching down and crossing over the river before climbing up around

*Not the best location for this sign.*

Monk's Moor. A sweet descent brings you down into Middleton in Teesdale. Here there are pubs, cafes and shops where you can refuel for your return leg.

Join the B6277 making your way up Teesdale back towards Alston. A long climb with an easy gradient heads up through Langdon Beck. In the early stages of this climb you have some spectacular views down to the River Tees, the road rises up out of the valley and over the pass between Hardship Fell on your left and Three Pikes up to your right. A long downhill is a welcome relief and will bring you to the southern edge of Alston Moor. Another small climb leads up around the edge of the moor before descending back into Alston. Take care on the cobbles as you drop down through the village centre to the A686.

You will now retrace your steps climbing up passing the Hartside Cafe before picking up this superb descent back down towards Penrith.

*You can see the switchbacks as you roll along next to the river. The road continues to climb beyond them.*

# 38 HEXHAM 1: STANHOPE STONKER

**Start point:** Hexham railway station

**Grid ref:** NY 94001 64274

**Postcode:** NE46 1ET

**Total distance:** 88km

**Total elevation:** 1402m

**Max elevation:** 574m

## KEY CLIMBS

**From km 0 to km 2.2:** 111m climb over 2.2km

**From km 3.7 to km 12.5:** 234m climb over 8.8km

**From km 25 to km 30.5:** 230m climb over 5.5km

**From km 36.5 to km 55.8:** 368m climb over 19.3km

**From km 72 to km 75:** 98m climb over 3km

**Other key elevation gain:** From km 0 to km 30.5: elevation gain of 427m over 30.5km

**Exposure:** 4.5/5

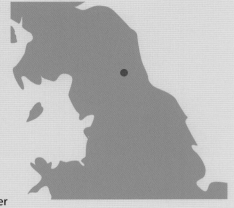

*Derwent Reservoir.*

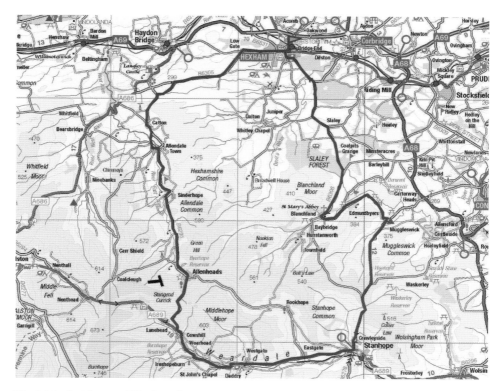

The historical town of Hexham is a starting point for a further two rides into the North Pennines. The town of Hexham itself is steeped in history. Its location close to the Scottish border means that the town has seen many battles throughout the border wars and was even burned down by William Wallace in 1297. There are many fantastic buildings in and around the town including the wonderful Hexham Abbey.

The first of two rides from Hexham will take you south through Slaley Forest and across Blanchland Moor. You will pass the stunning St Mary's Abbey before climbing up around Derwent Reservoir over Muggleswick Common and down to Stanhope, the route then heads west along Weardale before climbing up over Allendale Common northwards back to Hexham.

*Hidden valleys and winding roads lead you out to the open hill tops and big scenery.*

Climb up out of Hexham heading south on the B6306. The initial gradient is quite steep and can be a shock to those cold legs, so make sure to warm up beforehand.

**143**

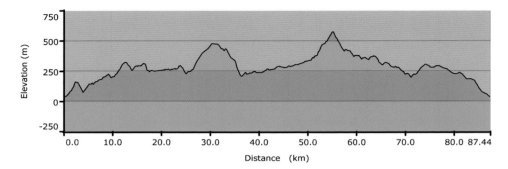

The road drops down a short but steep hill passing over a narrow stone bridge before climbing up along the edges of Dipton Wood. The asphalt rolls along, passing through Slaley Forest and out into the open of Blanchland Moor. You may get a sneaky peek of Derwent Reservoir over to

*Derwent Reservoir.*

your left as you descend down to Blanchland village.

Climb up through patchy pieces of woodland and around Edmundbyers Common with views down to the reservoir to your left. A tough section of open hilltop follows as you pass through Muggleswick Common heading south to Stanhope. A fast steep descent brings you down into the village to a T-junction where you take a right turn and make your way along Weardale. The road hugs the right-hand side of the valley and climbs uphill through Eastgate and Westgate onward to Cowshill. The landscape is littered with abandoned buildings, a reminder of man's never-ending struggle against the forces of nature.

Continue to climb on the B6295 passing through Allenheads and on to Allendale Town. Take a left in the town, crossing over the river and continuing to head northwards before crossing over the river once more. In a couple of kilometres you will reach a turning on your right for the B6304 back towards Hexham. This road joins into the B6305 and eventually leads you into a fast downhill back into town. Take care as you come into the town as there are multiple side roads and you pass a school. Back in the town centre simply retrace your steps back round to the railway station.

# 39 HEXHAM 2: HARTSIDE HAUL

**Start point:** Hexham railway station

**Grid ref:** NY 94001 64274

**Postcode:** NE46 1ET

**End point:** Penrith railway station

**Grid ref:** NY 51213 29894

**Postcode:** CA11 7JQ

**Alternative end point:** Langwathby railway station

**Grid ref:** NY 57321 33444

**Postcode:** CA10 1NZ

**Total distance:** 68km

**Total elevation:** 1146m

**Max elevation:** 574m

## KEY CLIMBS

**From km 0 to km 11.2:** 252m climb over 11.2km

**From km 18 to km 30:** 303m climb over 12 km

**From km 36.5 to km 45.5:** 295m climb over 9km

**Other key elevation gain:** From km 0 to km 45.5: elevation gain of 531m over 45.5km

**Exposure:** 4.5/5

The second ride from Hexham is one of a few point-to-point rides throughout the book. You have the choice of using the rail network to link back round from either Penrith or Lanwathby via Carlisle or you could simply make the turn in Penrith and retrace your steps back to your start point in Hexham.

Another option is to start from Carlisle and take the train to Hexham. From here

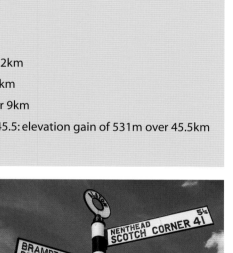

*Halfway.*

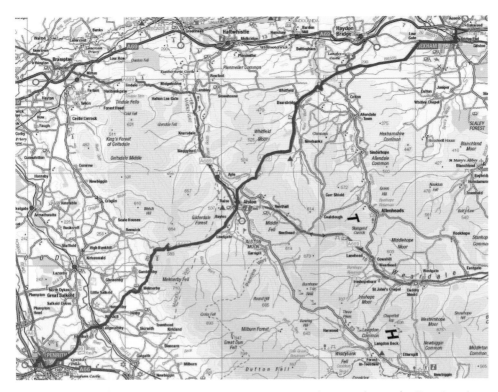

*Switching down to the River Allen, a rare series of switchbacks gives this section an Alpine feel.*

you can ride up and over the Pennines into Penrith (or stop earlier in Lanwathaby) and take the train back up to Carlisle, however, should you choose to ride back to Carlisle the section of road that links Penrith to Carlisle isn't particularly exciting. Don't forget that you can also link from Penrith across into the Lake District via one of my Windermere routes (see pages 120–128), making for a true epic ride.

From Hexham town centre, head west climbing up on the B6305. A junction on your right will take you past the village of Langley on the B6305 down to a T-junction with the A686. Here take a left turn and head towards a sweet little downhill that takes you through a series of switchbacks and down to the River Allen. Cross the river over a narrow bridge and climb up

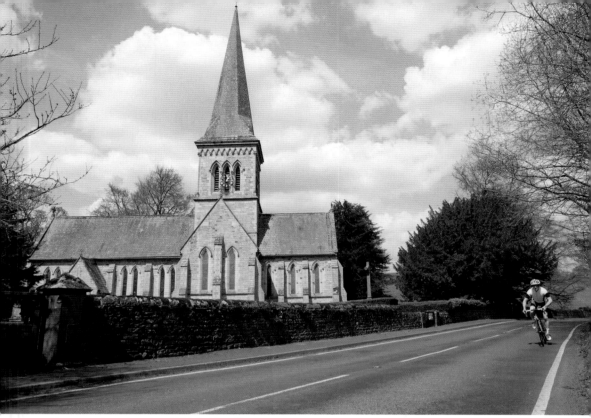

*The stunning church at Whitfield Hall.*

through the woodland towards Whitfield Hall.

You will now start the long but gradual climb up around Whitfield Moor, which will link you to a superb descent that brings you down through the trees into the town of Alston. There are some fantastic sequences of corners on this descent. The road is smooth and wide, enabling you to carry some good momentum. You will start to climb up as you leave Alston. The gradient is reasonably mellow and the climb very pleasurable.

As you crest the hill past the Hartside Cafe, start to make your descent down towards Penrith. This is another fantastic section of road as the premium asphalt winds its way down the hillside through

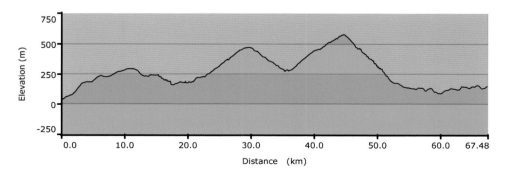

*Corners galore on the sweeping descent down from the Hartside Cafe.*

a patch of woodland and out into open farmland in the valley below. If you get the chance to take your eyes off the road you will see some spectacular views of the Lake District in the distance.

In several kilometres you will come to the village of Lanwathby. Here you can pick up a train that will take you to Carlisle. Alternatively, continue along the A686 and bear right into Penrith town centre, pick-

ing up signs for the railway station where you can catch a train back to Hexham via Carlisle. Once here in Penrith you will find all the usual amenities so if you choose to make an overnight stop and return the following day you have a wide choice of accommodation, from bed and breakfasts to luxury hotels. If you're feeling keen you could simply refuel, turn around and head back the way you've come.

# THE
# SCOTTISH
# BORDERS

# 40 DUMFRIES: DALBEATTIE DASH

**Start point:** Dumfries railway station

**Grid ref:** NX 97580 76490

**Postcode:** DG1 1NF

**Total distance:** 68.5km

**Total elevation:** 670m

**Max elevation:** 160m

## KEY CLIMBS

**From km 41 to km 57:** 150m climb over 16km

**Exposure:** 3/5

This short loop is frequently used by locals and has featured in the Tour of Britain as well as in the latest series of the British Road Race Championships. The route follows the Solway Coast, passing through the picturesque village of New Abbey and underneath Criffel before traversing above Mersehead Sands in the Solway Estuary. The route then hits the undulating coast line, passing through Sandy Hills Bay and round to Dalbeattie Forest. You will pass through 'the granite town' of Dalbeattie,

*The Solway Firth.*

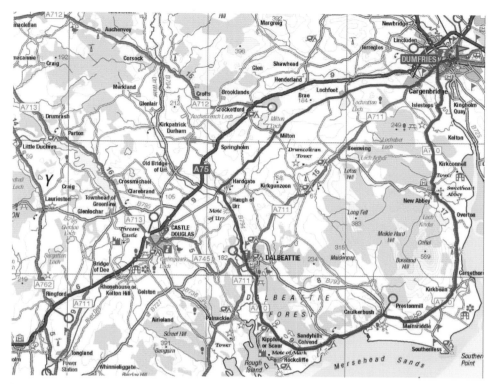

heading inland to pick up the old military road linking Dumfries to Castle Douglas. The rolling Dumfriesshire farmland that surrounds you as you head back towards the town makes for a pleasant end to this short but tough loop.

From the railway station, head along Lovers' Walk to the traffic lights. Here you take a left turn and head around the northern end of Dumfries town centre. Dropping down over the Buccleuch Bridge cross the River Nith before taking a left turn on the Solway coastal route towards New Abbey.

Beyond the town the road is relatively flat and gives you a chance to warm up the legs before the first climb past Mabie Forest up and over to the village of New Abbey, a mellow descent that leads you down into the village where you will pass The Old Mill and the remains of the Sweetheart Abbey. From New Abbey continue to follow the coast road (A710) around the southern flanks of Criffel with the estuary out on your left. On a clear day you can see across the estuary into the heart of the Lake District.

*Sweetheart Abbey.*

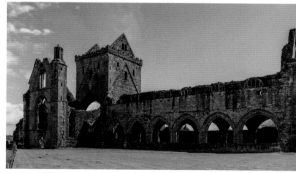

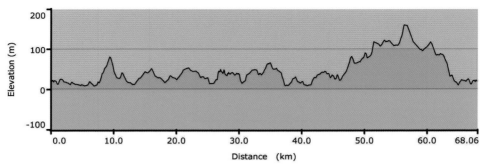

After the village of Caulkerbush the road starts to climb up. Between here and Sandy Hills lie a series of small rollers. Use the free speed from the descents to help propel you up the short but steep climbs. Throughout this section you get more spectacular views out across the estuary as you rise up and drop down along the cliff tops. The road passes through Sandy Hills and starts to move inland away from the coast. Climbing up gradually to Colvend, here you pass the White Loch and the southern tip of Dalbeattie Forest.

The road continues to wind its way along and has some great movement as it dips up and down through a few small sharp gradients. Over to your left lie the villages of Kippford and Rockcliffe. These

*Great views of the Solway Coast as you head to Sandyhills Bay.*

picturesque coastal villages are worth a visit if you fancy a break from the main route. The route continues in a northerly direction past the entrance to Dalbeattie Forest and on up to the town. You'll notice the fields are littered with large outcrops of white and pinkish granite, something the area is famed for.

*The road to Haugh of Urr heads inland, linking you to the old military road.*

In Dalbeattie, cross over the main A711 and continue heading north on the B794 towards Haugh of Urr. In the village take a right turn on to the old military road. You'll pass through lush rolling green country-side and a few small villages as you head back in a north-easterly direction towards Dumfries. On the outskirts of Dumfries you will pass through the small village of Cargenbridge. Follow the A711 back into the town centre, linking into your outward-bound section when you cross the River Nith.

# 41 LOCKERBIE 1: MOFFAT MISSION

**Start point:** Lockerbie railway station

**Grid ref:** NY 13625 81730

**Postcode:** DG11 2HA

**Total distance:** 115km

**Total elevation:** 1352m

**Max elevation:** 384m

## KEY CLIMBS

**From km 4 to km 40.5:** 278m climb over 41.5km

**From km 57 to km 63:** 155m climb over 6km

**From km 73 to km 81:** 115m climb over 7km

**From km 91.5 to km 94:** 98m climb over 2.5km

**Other key elevation gain:** From km 4 to km 63: elevation gain of 324m over 59km

**Exposure:** 4/5

The first of two loops to head out from Lockerbie heads northwards towards Moffat. You will then head off into the picturesque Moffat Dale, passing the large waterfall of Grey Mare's Tail before climbing over a pass descending down to St Mary's Loch. The road skirts around the edge of the picturesque loch before climbing up into Craik Forest and on through Eskdalemuir Forest. You will pass the Tibetan monastery at Samye Ling before returning through Castle O'er Forest back to Lockerbie. There are some absolutely fantastic sections of road offering superb views and great riding.

*There are many amazing roads in the Borders, stunning scenery and rarely a car to be seen.*

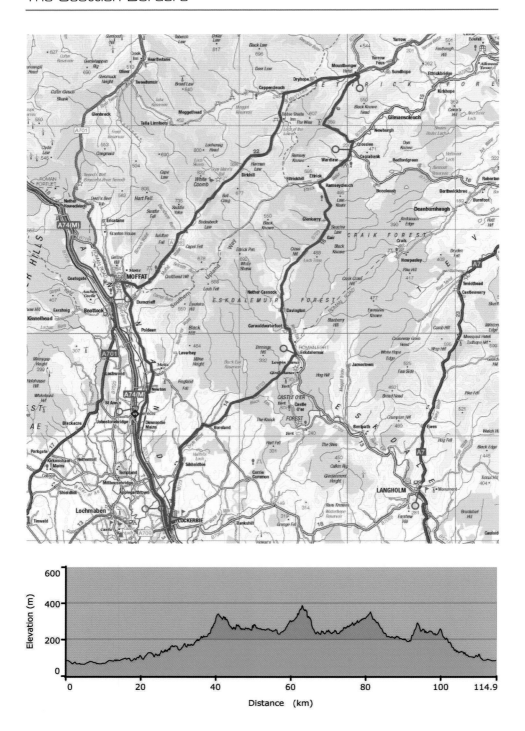

*The undulating road to St Mary's Loch will keep you entertained.*

From Lockerbie, head north on the B7068 joining the B7076. This section of road runs alongside the railway and motorway heading northwards towards Moffat. The opening sections are reasonably uneventful but they do give you a chance to warm up before you head out into the hills proper. At Dinwoodie Mains, take a right turn on to a minor road and head up through the village of Wamphray Gate and on to Craigbeck, joining into the A708 Moffat to Selkirk Road.

This spectacular section of road undulates and twist its way up the hillside running parallel to Moffat Water as you head in a north-easterly direction towards the town of Selkirk. Many sections of this road have been resurfaced and it really is a pleasure to ride. Further along on your left-hand side you will see the stunning waterfall of Grey Mare's Tail.

The road then climbs uphill on the right-hand side of the valley and leads you into a long flowing descent down to Loch of the Lowes and St Mary's Loch. Dipping in and out of the trees the road runs along the western flanks of the lochs and the views of the surrounding countryside are magnificent. A few kilometres after you leave the loch you will come to a public house on the left-hand side called the Gordon Arms Hotel.

Here, take a right turn at the crossroads passing over Yarrow Water and climbing uphill on the B709 underneath Meg's Hill. This steady climb will lead you up into the Craik Forest. Before you get to the forest, descend slightly down to Ettrick Water. Here the road takes a right turn and starts heading in a southerly direction towards the village of Ettrick. You will pass through the westerly fringes of the Craik Forest.

*Classic Dumfries & Galloway, they say to wait 20 minutes or move 20 miles for the weather to change – four seasons in one day is not uncommon in these parts.*

*The flat sections beside the loch allow the legs to recover before the climb up into the Craik Forest.*

Beyond the forest, you will pass a seismological station to your left-hand side before entering Eskdalemuir Forest.

The narrow lane continues to twist and wind its way along through the forest and you will pass the Samye Ling Tibetan Centre on your left-hand side. Here there is a cafe where you can take on refreshments, and you're welcome to wonder around the centre and surrounding gardens.

The smooth undulating narrow road continues for a couple of kilometres beyond the Tibetan Centre into Eskdalemuir, here take a right turn on to the B723 back towards Lockerbie. This stunning section of road – a real treat – dips down and climbs up several times while snaking its way through forests and open hilltops. Watch out for the logging trucks as these guys stop for no man or beast! On these final few kilometres you will pass through Castle O'er Forest and the magnificent Lockerbie Manor.

# 42 LOCKERBIE 2: TIBETAN TWIST

**Start point:** Lockerbie railway station

**Grid ref:** NY 13625 81730

**Postcode:** DG11 2HA

**Total distance:** 72km

**Total elevation:** 1040m

**Max elevation:** 284m

## KEY CLIMBS

**From km 0 to km 20.8:** 202m climb over 20.8km

**From km 26 to km 27.8:** 95m climb over 1.8km

**From km 44 to km 54:** 154m climb over 10km

**Exposure:** 4/5

*Samye Ling Tibetan centre.*

The second and shorter loop from Lockerbie takes you out through Castle O'er Forest to the village of Eskdalemuir. Here just off the loop you will find the Samye Ling Tibetan Centre. The route heads east through Eskdale, running alongside the River Esk towards the town of Langholm. This fantastic stretch of road snakes its way through the undulating hills, offering spectacular views of the surrounding countryside. From Langholm the route heads back towards Lockerbie, twisting in and around small woodlands and dipping up and down through this wonderful part of the Scottish Borders.

From the train station in Lockerbie, head on to the high street, taking a right turn and heading north. Bear right on to the B723 heading towards Eskdalemuir. The road runs along the valley on some smooth fast-rolling asphalt up to the village of Boreland. You will now start to climb up into the hills towards Castle O'er Forest. There are some lovely views all around and you get to see this fine smooth strip of asphalt snake its way through the landscape in front of you.

*Smooth asphalt leads you out to Eskdalemuir.*

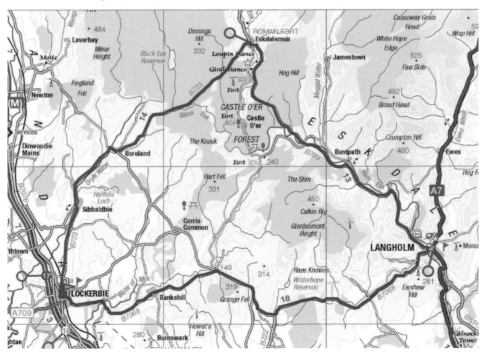

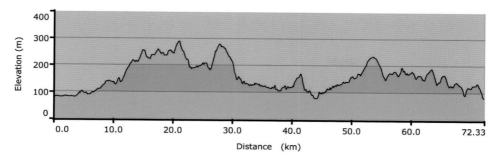

In Eskdalemuir the route takes a right turn heading towards Langholm. If you wish to investigate the Tibetan Samye Ling Centre then take a left turn and follow the road for a few kilometres where you will see the Tibetan Centre on your right-hand side. Here there is a cafe and ornamental gardens which you are free to walk around.

From Eskdalemuir village pick up the B709 signposted towards Langholm. This fantastic stretch of road passes through the eastern flanks of Castle O'er Forest and follows the River Esk down to Langholm. Just before you reach the river in the town centre take a right turn on to the B7068 back towards Lockerbie. This junction is just past the school but is poorly signposted so be careful not to miss it. If you reach the river you have gone too far.

The narrow road makes its way out of Langholm in a south-westerly direction following Wauchope Water. Here, the lush green countryside and small patches of woodland are pleasing to the eye, the road itself is full of interesting movement as it dips up and down twisting around small farmsteads crossing many burns (streams) as you make your way back towards Lockerbie.

*Fast descents on super-smooth asphalt. Dumfries & Galloway has some fantastic roads.*

*The undulating road from Langholm links back through open countryside to Lockerbie.*

# 43 MOFFAT: MOFFAT MASH-UP

**Start point:** Moffat town centre

**Grid ref:** NT 08513 05262

**Postcode:** DG10 9ED

**Total distance:** 70.5km

**Total elevation:** 1180m

**Max elevation:** 461m

## KEY CLIMBS

**From km 0 to km 11:** 308m climb over 11km

**From km 30.5 to km 32.5:** 167m climb over 2km

**Other key elevation gain:** From km 0 to km 32.5: elevation gain of 340m

**Exposure:** 4.5/5

*Megget Reservoir.*

The fourth ride in the Scottish Borders starts from the market town of Moffat. From the town of Moffat, you will climb up around the Devil's Beef Tub past the source of the River Tweed and River Annan, then heading north following the River Tweed towards the village of Tweedsmuir. You will then climb up past Talla Reservoir on a tough climb used in the 2012 Tour of Britain and on to Megget Reservoir. Join St Mary's Loch and head southwards back towards Moffat, climbing up over the pass and dropping back down before passing the spectacular Grey Mare's Tail waterfall, This superb section of road winds its way along Moffat Dale back towards the town. There are plenty of stunning views, stiff climbs and superb downhills to keep you entertained.

*The Devil's Beef Tub.*

From Moffat town centre head north climbing up through the woodland and into open ground with the valley to your right and the high peak of Hart Fell in the

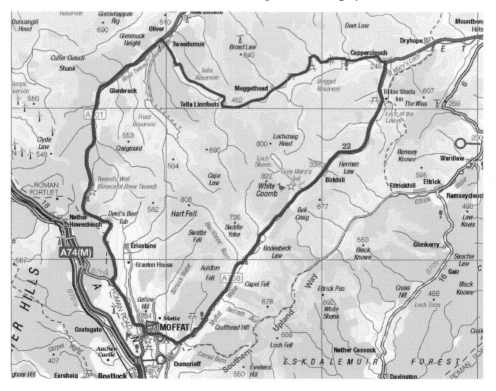

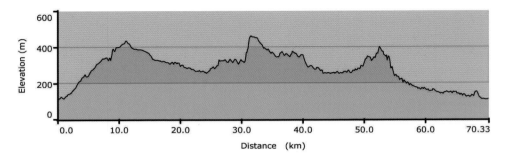

distance. The climb up to the Devil's Beef Tub may last for several kilometres but the gradients are very easy. Passing the monument at Ericstane, you round the Devil's Beef Tub. Apparently, this was a favoured spot for hiding cattle during the border raids.

The road drops down through woodland and you come out into open ground running alongside the River Tweed. In the village of Tweedsmuir take a right turn, dropping down and crossing the river

before heading up through the woodland towards the dam at the end of Talla Reservoir. The narrow road runs alongside the reservoir clinging to Muckle Side Hill. This steep-sided valley is quite imposing and leads you to a stiff climb with some severe gradient linking the two reservoirs.

As you crest the hill the road makes its way across a few kilometres of open hilltop between rocky outcrops before coming to the end of Megget Reservoir. Once again the road runs along the edge of the

*The steep climb between the two reservoirs.*

*A superb descent leads you down into Moffat Dale passing the Grey Mare's Tail.*

reservoir, clinging to the hillside before descending down to a junction with the A708 Moffat to Selkirk Road. Here, take a right-hand turn and run along the western side of St Mary's Loch. Within a few kilometres, leave the loch behind and start to climb up in open ground past Paper Hill up to your right and Herman Law towering above you over to your left.

A fast but narrow descent drops down to the Grey Mare's Tail waterfall on your right-hand side. There are two narrow bridges just below the waterfall and it is worth stopping to take a quick look up to your right. The newly laid super-smooth asphalt unwinds in front of you as you pass through the valley base and run along Moffat Dale. The road is very undulating and takes in a few climbs that will deal tired legs a blow. One final rise links you into the small descent back into the town of Moffat.

*Watch for rocks being washed on to the road.*

# 44 SANQUHAR: LEADHILLS LEG BURNER

**Start point:** Sanquhar railway station

**Grid ref:** NS 78162 10277

**Postcode:** DG4 6DQ

**Total distance:** 68km

**Total elevation:** 952m

**Max elevation:** 465m

## KEY CLIMBS

**From km 17 to km 32:** 282m climb over 15km

**From km 41 to km 52:** 195m climb over 11km

**Other key elevation gain:** From km 17 to km 52: elevation gain of 398m over 35km

**Exposure:** 5/5

Located to the west of the Lowther Hills lies the town of Sanquhar, this is the start point for a ride that takes in some spectacular scenery and stunning roads. Heading southwards towards the town of Dumfries then up into the hills through the Dalveen Pass, this magnificent valley is a grand opening for a grand ride. Beyond the pass a smooth strip of asphalt winds its way across open ground towards the small village of Elvanfoot. Here the route heads back west towards the old mining town of Leadhills and Wanlockhead. You then enter another magnificent valley and descend down through the Mennock Pass.

From the railway station in Sanquhar head south on the A76 towards Dumfries. The opening section descends down into a valley following the railway and the River Nith. You will pass Drumlanrig Castle on your right-hand side. It's worth a diversion to go and take a look at the magnificent castle, which is also home to a bicycle museum. Back on route, take a minor road opposite the entrance to Drumlanrig

*Bicycle museum at Drumlanrig Castle.*

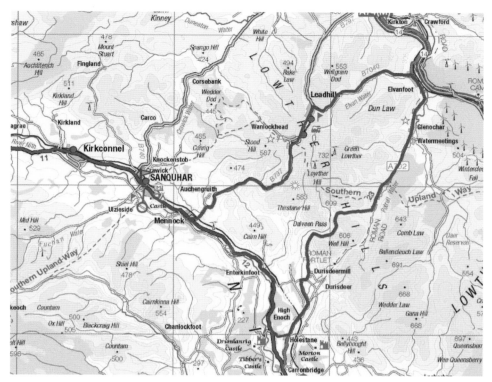

Castle linking you on to the A702 where you head north towards the Dalveen Pass.

The large rolling hills above Durisdeer hide a Roman road and fortlet. This area of the Scottish Borders has seen a lot of action over the years and the surrounding fields are littered with archaeology. Enter the Dalveen Pass and the road hugs the right-hand side of the valley as you climb up and around the large rolling green hillsides. An old metal railing lines the road as you pass over the brightly painted black and white bridges past the fast-flowing waters from the hills above.

You will crest the hill and come out into open moorland. Here, a superb stretch of super-smooth fast-rolling asphalt unfolds across the open moorland and into the small village of Elvanfoot. The road drops

*Quiet, smooth, stunning scenery: Dumfries & Galloway is a well-kept secret full of stunning roads.*

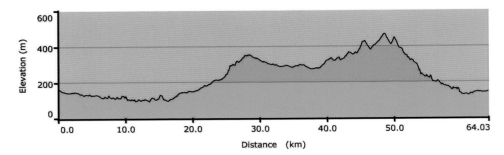

*The link back to Leadhills where more surprise sections of road await you.*

down and takes a tight right-hand switch over a bridge climbing up and out. At the top of the small rise, take a left turn towards Leadhills and Wanlockhead.

The quiet road runs alongside Elvan Water in open countryside before climbing up around Broad Law hill and descending down into Leadhills village. Here there is a museum documenting the history of the area and a narrow gauge railway where enthusiasts gather to keep a fleet of old mining locomotives and wagons running.

The route then climbs up and over a small hill before descending down through a lovely series of corners and through the village of Wanlockhead. Beyond the village a small climb leads you into the Mennock Pass.

*The road through the Mennock Pass is quite spectacular.*

A superb downhill drops into a valley, hugging the hills on the right-hand side and snaking alongside an old metal guard rail. In the valley base the large rounded hills tower above you as you make your way back towards the main A76 at Mennock village. Here you rejoin the main road and head back upwards to the start point in Sanquhar.

# SCOTLAND, THE CENTRAL BELT

# 45 LINLITHGOW: BEECRAIGS BLAST

**Start point:** Linlithgow railway station

**Grid ref:** NT 00473 77036

**Postcode:** EH49 7DH

**Total distance:** 35.5km

**Total elevation:** 590m

**Max elevation:** 292m

## KEY CLIMBS

**From km 1 to km 4.8:** 185m climb over 3.8km

**From km 15.5 to km 20.5:** 150m climb over 5km

**Exposure:** 3/5

Linlithgow is located to the west of Edinburgh in West Lothian. Famed for its spectacular palace, the town is also the birthplace of James V and Mary, Queen of Scots. This small but busy town is the start point for one of three rides in the central belt. The route takes you up into the hills

*The winding roads are superb fun – short stiff climbs and plenty of good movement.*

to the south of the town through some wonderful undulating twisty roads around Beecraigs Country Park. There are some spectacular views down to the River Forth and on a clear day you can see the famous Forth Rail Bridge in the distance. There are many rocky outcrops and viewpoints along the route.

The route starts by heading in a westerly direction along Linlithgow High Street. Look out for the brown tourist signs to Beecraigs Country Park and take the left turn climbing up out of the town.

The road climbs up through a series of switchbacks before cresting the hill and running round with open countryside out to your right and the country park to your left. Over in the distance you can see the ancient hill fort at Cockleroy. Over the next

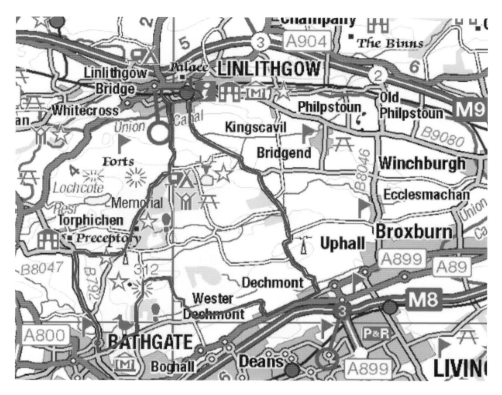

few kilometres the road dips down and climbs up several times, twisting its way around the edge of the country park. Just below Cairnpapple Hill, take a fork to the right and descend down a fast section of smooth asphalt into Torphichen village.

At the crossroads in the village take a left turn heading in a southerly direction towards the town of Bathgate on B792. Down in Bathgate a left turn leads you east to a crossroads where the route takes a left turn climbing up Bathgate Hills to a viewpoint at Knock. Here you are at an elevation of 310 metres. The route then descends down off of the hill through

*Freshly laid asphalt on the descent to Torphichen.*

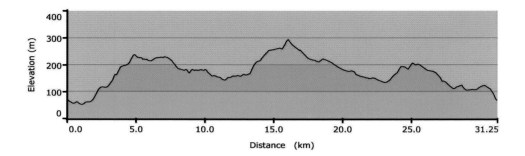

a series of tight turns to a crossroads at Drumcross, where you will take a left turn.

You then join the A89 for a short section before forking off to the left into the village of Dechmont. Just before you exit the village take a left turn and climb up back on to the hill heading into a north-westerly direction towards Beecraigs Country Park.

You will pass Riccarton Hills on your left-hand side before descending through the small village of Riccarton into the final rise that leads you back over the hill down into Linlithgow. Take care at the bottom of the hill in the town as the road narrows over the canal and takes a tight right turn back to the railway station.

*The smooth undulating road makes its way around Beecraigs Country Park.*

# 46 LONGNIDDRY: GOLFERS GALORE

*Berwick Law in the background as you head back West.*

**Start point:** Longniddry railway station near Edinburgh

**Grid ref:** NT 44585 76262

**Postcode:** EH32 0LS

**Total distance:** 34km

**Total elevation:** 196m

**Max elevation:** 78m

## KEY CLIMBS

**From km 16 to km 20:** 73m climb over 4km

**Other key elevation gain:** From km 5.5 to km 20.5: elevation gain of 75m over 15km

**Exposure:** 3/5

The second loop in the Edinburgh region starts to the east of the city centre from the village of Longniddry. You will ride along the coast following the southern banks of the Firth of Forth passing Gosforth Bay, Aberlady Bay and Gullane Bay as you head towards North Berwick. Just off the route at Dirleton lies the remains of the castle, which is well worth a visit. From North Berwick you head south, passing North

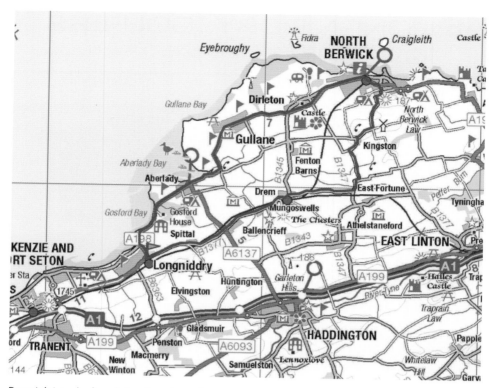

Berwick Law before following the railway line back to Longniddry. The opening sections of this loop are often used by local riders for a quick blast after work or at the

*Scottish sandstone, a gatehouse to Gosford House.*

weekends. The road is also a great way to access the Lammermuir Hills. Here there are some stiff climbs and stunning views. Should you wish to extend your route, we have laced together a short but interesting loop with coastal views and quiet roads all easily accessible from the city centre itself.

From the train station, head in a northerly direction to the A198 coast road. Here take a right turn heading in an easterly direction towards North Berwick, passing Gosford Bay. There are views back towards the city before bearing right to the village of Aberlady. Once again the road hugs the coastline before skirting through the dunes and weaving through the multiple golf courses up to Gullane. To the south side of the village lies the remains of a castle and a dismantled railway, a common

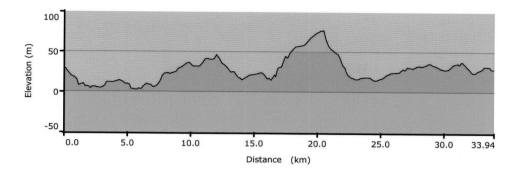

theme on the majority of routes through-out the book.

As you head east the main road skirts around the village of Dirleton. Within the village itself lies the remains of a castle, built from the local sandstone; it's an impressive building and worth a quick diversion through the village centre to take a look. When you arrive in the town of North Berwick you have the option of heading into the town centre itself on to the seafront or bearing right continuing

on the A198 and climbing up around the south side of the town. Look for the B1347 which will continue to climb up past the old hill fort of North Berwick Law, this is clearly signposted to Haddington and the National Museum of Flight.

The road winds its way through small villages in open countryside offering some great views and fast-rolling asphalt. If you want, you could always take a break from riding and head over to the National Museum of Flight. The route takes a right

*Coastal views as you leave the city behind.*

*Smooth roads and small hills make for fast riding. North Berwick Law in the background is a prominent feature.*

*The final leg to the railway station.*

turn just before a railway bridge (this is where you can continue straight on between the villages of Haddington and East Linton out into the hills) and runs along next to the railway back to the start point of Longniddry railway station. Just beyond the village of Drem lies a small motor museum, another worthy stop if you're not on a fast training ride.

# CENTRAL SCOTLAND

# 47 MILNGAVIE: JAMIE'S JEWEL

**Start point:** Milngavie railway station

**Grid ref:** NS 55632 74402

**Postcode:** G62 8PG

**Total distance:** 54km

**Total elevation:** 757m

**Max elevation:** 340m

## KEY CLIMBS

**From km 0 to km 3.5:** 95m climb over 3.5km

**From km 23 to km 33.5:** 272m climb over 10.5km

**Other key elevation gain:** From km 12 to km 33.5: elevation gain of 302m over 21.5km

**Exposure:** 4/5

We have another classic lined up for you in Scotland's central belt with a short but tough route heading out through the Campsie Fells from the outskirts of

*You pass a traditional distillery on the return leg, temping to have a tipple.*

Glasgow. This route is a particular favourite with locals, taking in rolling roads, stunning scenery and a good climb up over the main fells, leading into a fast descent back down off the hills. Some of the sections of road have a rough surface so choose your tyres and wheels wisely.

From the railway station, pick up the A81 heading north pass the Craigmaddie Reservoir. This undulating early section of road is a great start to a great loop. The main road should be approached with caution throughout the busier times of day as commuters cut in and out of the city.

Passing through Strathblane, continue heading in a northerly direction on the main road. You'll pass the Strathblane

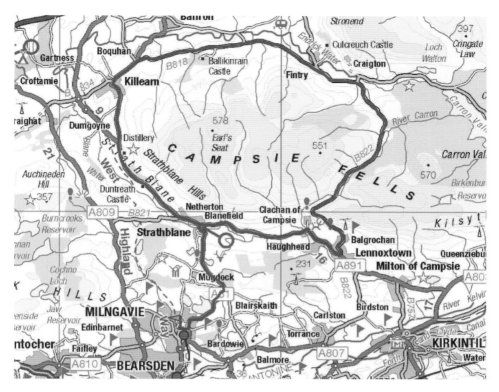

The fast descent and smooth surface is a welcome relief from the harsh outbound roads and open hilltop sections.

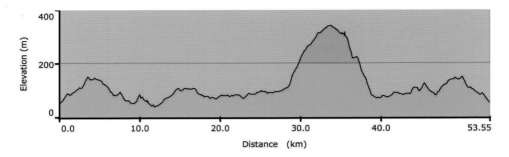

*Waterfalls and running water are a common theme on the Scottish rides.*

hills out to your right and circumnavigate around the Campsie Fells to the northern flanks. Having passed the distillery (avoiding the temptations that lie within) take a fork off to your right on to the A875 towards Killearn. Passing through the small village follow the road and within a couple of kilometres fork right on to the B818. This undulating road makes its way along the northern flanks of the Campsie Fells and offers some spectacular views of the surrounding countryside.

The river Endrick Water meanders along the valley to your left as you pass through small woodlands and open ground up to the village of Fintry. Just beyond the village in a few kilometres the road bears round to the right and starts to climb uphill over Campsie Muir. You will pass over the open moorland hilltop on a steady gradient before you start to descend through a valley down to Allenhead. It's down here on a tight left-hand corner you will encounter spectacular views down Campsie Glen to Jamie Wright's Well.

The fast descent continues to traverse the hillside down to a tight right-hand corner into Lennoxtown. Here you take a right turn and head west towards Strathblane. In the village pick up the A81 and retrace your steps along the rolling road to Milngavie.

# 48 DUNBLANE: DANCE OF THE NAUGHTY KNIGHT

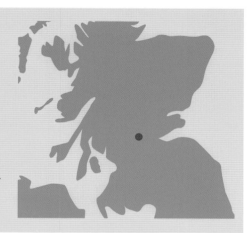

**Start point:** Dunblane railway station

**Grid ref:** NN 78018 00967

**Postcode:** FK15 9ET

**Total distance:** 72km

**Total elevation:** 895m

**Max elevation:** 260m

## KEY CLIMBS

**From km 28 to km 33:** 226m climb over 5km

**Exposure:** 3.5/5

This superb loop takes in the spectacular Duke's Pass. You will also pass through Doune where you will find the castle that was featured in the film *Monty Python and the Holy Grail*. Beyond Doune, head west passing Flanders Moss on the undulating road to Aberfoyle. You will pass the Lake of Menteith to the south side of Menteith Hills to Aberfoyle. With its various cafes this small town is the start to a great climb up and over the Duke's Pass. This spectacular road makes its way through woodland across to the edge of the Trossachs National Park before heading east along the shores of Loch Venachar to the town of Callander. Then, pick up the back roads heading along next to the River Teith passing back through Doune on to Dunblane.

From the railway station pick up the A820 heading west towards Doune. As you enter the village you will see the brown tourist signs pointing to the castle on your

*The castle near Doune in all its splendour.*

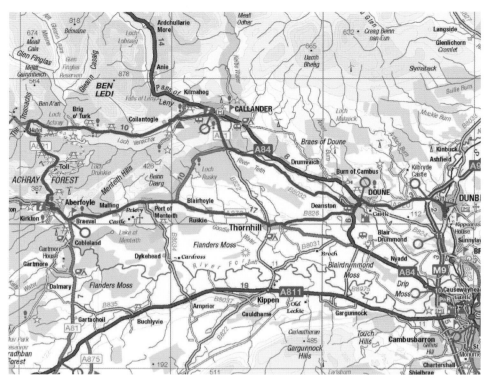

left-hand side. If you're a Monty Python fan you simply have to pay a visit to the spectacular castle where John Cleese shouted insults to the knights below in *Monty Python and the Holy Grail*. Your holy grail is the Duke's Pass and to get there head south from Doune on the main A84 before picking up the B826 signposted to Aberfoyle, take care on the main road as it can get quite busy at times.

The undulating B road passes through the village of Thornhill and links you on to to the A873 where you will continue west joining the A81 to Aberfoyle. In Aberfoyle you get the chance to pick up some refreshments before making your climb up the winding road through Aberfoyle Forest and on to the hilltops. This really is a spectacular section of road, the smooth asphalt makes its way up through the hills

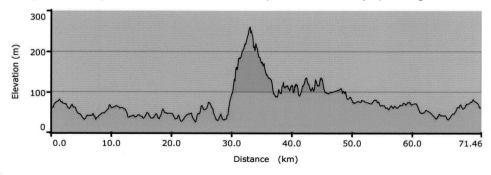

*The Duke's Pass is a majestic strip of asphalt.*

*Carry speed through the corners and make light work of the climbs.*

and you get some spectacular views of the surrounding scenery as the many corners link between one another.

A fast downhill leads you to Loch Achray where you will follow the shoreline before heading east passing through

*Granite Grandeur of An Tigh Mor.*

Brig o' Turk and on to the shores of Loch Venachar. This road forms part of the Trossachs National Park scenic drive and can become cluttered with tourists throughout the peak season.

At the Loch end take a right turn on a minor road cutting through to the south side of Callander, from here climb up on the A81 for a couple of kilometres before swinging left on to the B8032. This undulating road passes through woodland with the River Teith running in the valley to your left bringing you back to the main A84 near Doune. The return leg back to Dublane railway station simply retraces the steps of your outward bound journey.

# 49 TARBET: THE REST & BE THANKFUL

**Start point:** Arrochar & Tarbet railway station

**Grid ref:** NN 31178 04457

**Postcode:** G83 7DB

**Total distance:** 152km

**Total elevation:** 2448m

**Max elevation:** 298m

## KEY CLIMBS

**Out:**

**From km 3 to km 14:** 293m climb over 11km

**From km 39 to km 45.5:** 114m climb over 6.5km

**Return:**

**From km 102 to km 106.5:** 114m climb over 4.5km

**From km 128 to km 138:** 293m climb over 10km

**Exposure:** 4/5

*Stunning Scottish scenery.*

This monster out-and-back ride covers just over 150 kilometres and nearly 2500 metres of climbing. Should you wish to do so you could always make an overnight stop and head back the following day. A superb selection of asphalt runs through some stunning scenery: passing up and over the Rest & Be Thankful, having climbed up Glen Croe, the route then joins the head of Glen Fyne and heads around to Inveraray past Stirling Castle and southwards along the shores of Loch Fyne to Lochgilphead. Here make a U-turn and retrace your steps along this super stretch of asphalt in the Scottish Highlands.

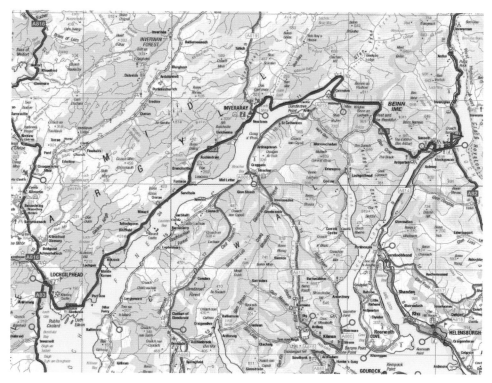

*The long climb up to the Rest & Be Thankful.*

This route starts at the small railway station to the western side of Loch Lomond. Follow the main A83 to Lochgilphead. Even though this is marked as a major trunk road it doesn't ever get that busy. There is plenty of good visibility and room for vehicles to pass. Round the hill and pass through the village of Arrochar at the north end of Loch Long. The road hugs the shoreline before swinging right, climbing up through Ardgartan Forest along Glen Croe.

A long but mellow climb leads up to the saddle of the Rest & Be Thankful. Then a long descent drops down next to Loch Restil and into Glen Kinglas. Hugging the hillsides, snake your way around and join the north-easterly tip of Loch Fyne. This huge body of water stretches out before

*Tough climbs are rewarded with superb descents and epic scenery.*

the eye as you continue on what was the old military road into Inveraray.

You will leave the loch side for several kilometres as you climb up through the forest before descending back down to the water's edge at Furnace. Once again follow along the loch side to the village of Minard before another brief excursion away from the loch takes you up through woodland before dropping down to Lochgair village.

The road continues in a similar vein, cutting up and away from the loch and climbing up over small hills on its way

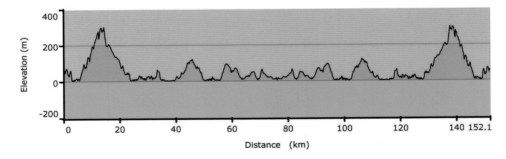

*The return leg up the Rest & Be Thankful.*

to the halfway point and turn at Lochgilphead. Here you will have the chance to refuel before making the turn and heading back. As you will have already seen, there are going to be some tough climbs on the return leg to the station at Tarbet.

# SCOTLAND, HIGHLANDS

# 50 FORT WILLIAM: MOY AHOY

**Start point:** Fort William railway station

**Grid ref:** NN 10558 74139

**Postcode:** PH33 6TQ

**Total distance:** 73.5km

**Total elevation:** 922m

**Max elevation:** 295m

## KEY CLIMBS

**From km 0 to km 42:** 287m climb over 42km

**Exposure:** 4/5

Here is another Highland classic taking in some sweet climbs and flowing roads as you ride through the Grampian Mountains that link the towns of Fort William and Newtonmore. You could ride this as an out-and-back or simply do a point-to-point ride using the rail network to link you back to a start point of your choice (the line

*The route offers some amazing views of the Grampian Mountains.*

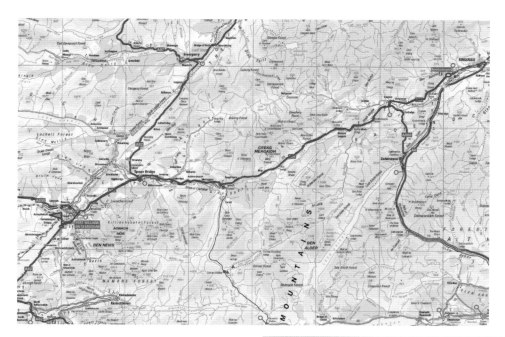

to Fort William runs from Glasgow and you can link back from Newtonmore to Glasgow, making this an ideal start point should you wish to use the train). The route climbs up through Glen Spean and Moy Forest passing along next to the beautiful Loch Laggan and on to Newtonmore via Laggan Forest.

From the railway station in Fort William head out in an easterly direction on the A82 towards Spean Bridge. In the village bear right on to the A86 following the river Spean. The opening sections are relatively flat and easy-going but don't be fooled as you will cover just under 1000 metres of climbing throughout the 73 kilometres.

From Spean Bridge the winding road makes its way up the glen through the forests past Tulloch Station and on to Loch Laggan. Here you roll along the northern side of the Loch below Aberarder Forest. This is a superb piece of road with great

*You may well need to go slow if you're to take this ride on as an out-and-back.*

scenery and great movement. At the far end of the loch you will come back into the trees and make your way through to the other side of the forest and into Laggan village.

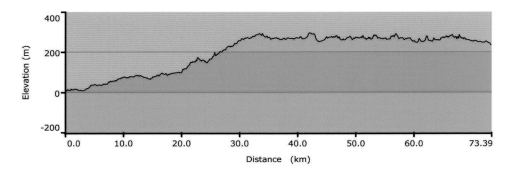

Out in open countryside the road runs along the valley base up towards the town of Newtonmore, where you take the right turn down to the railway station. Alternatively you can refuel and make the turn riding back to Fort William.

*Spectacular scenery at the roadside and in the distance.*

# 51 GLENFINNAN: WEST COAST WONDER

**Start point:** Glenfinnan railway station

**Grid ref:** NM 89855 80993

**Postcode:** PH37 4LS

**Total distance:** 130km

**Total elevation:** 2186m

**Max elevation:** 152m

## KEY CLIMBS

**From km 26.5 to km 30:** 142m climb over 3.5km

**From km 36 to km 38:** 102m climb over 4km

**From km 65.5 to km 73:** 124m climb over 7.5km

**Exposure:** 4/5

The West Coast of Scotland is full of spectacular scenery, with mystical lochs and glens. The stunning scenery hides many hidden treasures and amazing roads. The route takes you along the coast at the Sound of Arisaig before swinging inland, passing Loch Sunart and heading east through Glen Tarbet and on to the shores of Loch Linnhe. Then, head northwards following the loch side, passing through Inverscaddie Bay and back round to the start point of Glenfinnan railway station.

Starting from the beautifully refurbished period station the route picks up the A830 heading west following the railway line towards the small village of Lochailort passing Loch Eilt along the way. Here, pick up the coast road (A861) which

*Looking across Loch Linnhe.*

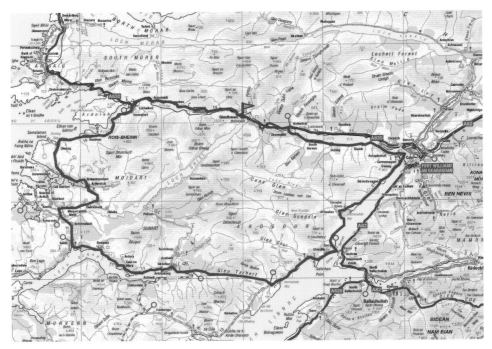

twists its way around the rocky shoreline on the Sound of Arisaig. On your right are jaw-dropping views towards the Isle of Eigg.

The road through Glenuig passes through woodland dropping down to Loch Moidart. The road hugs the shoreline and will narrow down into a single-track

*Spectacular coastal views on this route used in a classic Sportive.*

*Island views and winding roads.*

road. Visibility is relatively good and there are plenty of passing points should you encounter oncoming traffic.

The road continues to twist its way down towards the western tip of Loch Shiel. There are some sweet corners and undulations to the road and the surrounding scenery really is breathtaking. A short section links to the shore of Loch Sunart. The narrow road winds its way along the loch shore heading towards Glen Tarbet.

The glen road is not too shabby either. Here the road widens out and the towering peak of Meall a' Chuilinn looks down on you as you climb uphill, the glen road brings you down to the shores of Loch Linnhe. Once again the road hugs the shoreline. You will head north-eastwards along the loch's edge on single-track roads that cut through rocky outcrops. At the northern tip of the loch there are views across towards Fort William. The road swings round to the west and onwards to Loch Eil. Here, pick up the main A830 and run alongside the railway back to Glenfinnan.

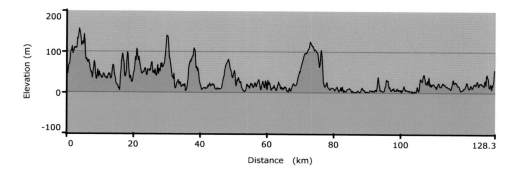

# 52 INVERNESS: IN SEARCH OF THE MONSTER

**Start point:** Inverness railway station

**Grid ref:** NH 66577 45516

**Postcode:** IV2 3PY

**Total distance:** 78.5km

**Total elevation:** 790m

**Max elevation:** 264m

## KEY CLIMBS

**From km 0 to km 11:** 245m climb over 11km

**Exposure:** 4/5

*The legendary Loch Ness.*

This route takes you out of the Highland city up past Leys Castle and across Drumossie Muir picking up quiet back roads past Loch Mhor around Farigaig Forest. The route then descends next to the River Foyers past the Falls of Foyers and down to the shores of the famous Loch Ness. Then follow the shoreline of the loch right the way back into Inverness city.

From the railway station, head northwards up the high street before swinging back on yourself. Running alongside the river on the B862, here you have lovely views over the city as you make your way out into the countryside. On the outskirts of the city you will come to a roundabout where you will take a left turn, skirting along the southern side of Inverness until reaching the third roundabout where you

*A short climb up from Inverness offers stunning views.*

will take a right turn on to the B861. You will come to a T-junction with a lack of signage. Just follow your nose, taking a right turn climbing uphill away from the built-up area.

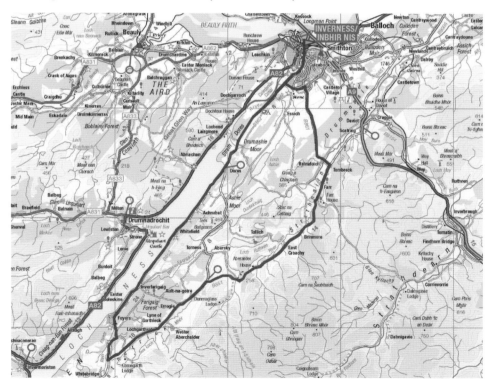

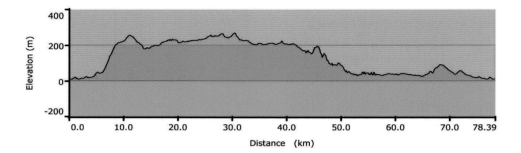

The opening climb has a few steep sections but offers some spectacular views out across the hills. You'll pass over the hilltop through woodland and descend down in open ground, passing the stone circle on your left-hand side. Nearing the bottom of the descent the road takes a series of tight corners before crossing over the River Nairn into the village of Tombreck. The route now picks up the B851 ahead in a southerly direction. This quiet back road is narrow with passing places and winds its way along with interesting movement both up and down passing around small woodlands.

At the village of Errogie you will rise up above Loch Mhor before descending down to a junction on your right for the B852. This fantastic stretch of road twists its way along through the woodland next to the River Foyers. It really is a spectacular section of road.

You will pass the Falls of Foyers. Unfortunately the waterfalls are not visible from

*The fields are littered with boulders. This large stane (stone) forms part of a sizable stone circle.*

*The most famous loch in Scotland. Good luck spotting a monster.*

the road and require a hike down some stairs to get a view, but if you have suitable footwear it's worth the walk down. On route, the road descends down past the village of Foyers on to General Wade's Military Road on the shores of Loch Ness.

The stunning vast loch leads you all the way back up to Inverness. There are spectacular views across the loch with ample opportunity to stop and savour them. This road lies in the shade for the first half of the day and temperatures can be quite cool down by the water's edge, particularly in the earlier and latter part of the year. When you arrive back in Inverness simply retrace your steps into the city centre back to the railway station.

*Leaving the loch behind you make your way back to Inverness.*

# 53 BEAULY: WE ARE GLASS

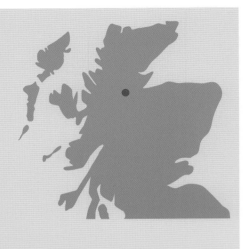

**Start point:** Beauly railway station

**Grid ref:** NH 52011 45831

**Postcode:** IV4 7EF

**Total distance:** 63km

**Total elevation:** 832m

**Max elevation:** 272m

## KEY CLIMBS

**From km 0 to km 15.5:** 265m climb over 15.5km

**From km 18.5 to km 32.5:** 164m climb over 14km

**Exposure:** 4/5

*The quiet town of Beauly in bloom.*

The second loop starting from the Inverness region begins just outside Inverness at the village of Beauly. Head out into the scenic Highland surroundings through Boblainy Forest along Glen Convinth to Glen Urquhart. A superb section of road takes you westwards to the River Glass at the small remote village of Cannich before heading along next to Balmore Forest up Strathglass. Here, follow the river up past Erchless Castle. The route around Ruttle

*Church ruins in Beauly.*

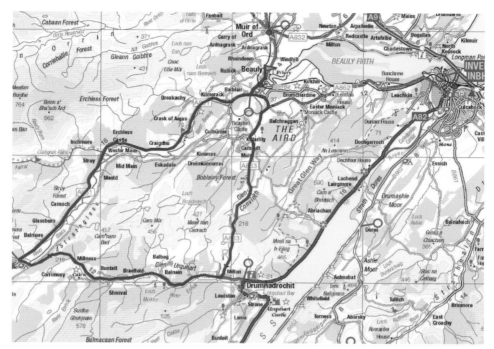

Wood joins the River Beauly back to the railway station in this picturesque Highland village.

From the railway station head south down to Lovat Bridge following the A862 back towards Inverness. In a few kilometres take a right turn on to the A833, heading in a southerly direction towards Glen Convinth. This opening section of road makes its way through woodland and across open ground before a fast, although slightly rough, downhill brings you into the village of Milton.

Head west, running along next to the River Enrick out into some epic scenery. As you head along the waterside up through Glen Urquhart you get a real sense of how remote this part of the British Isles is. The gradual climb brings you up to a fast downhill to the most westerly corner of the route into the village of Cannich, a right

*Highland scenery at its best.*

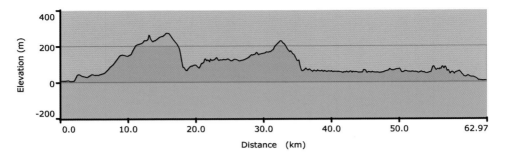

turn at a set of lights puts you on to the bridge over the River Glass before heading along the hillside making your way along Strathglass on a superb single-track road.

The views along the valley base are truly spectacular as you pass through small knotted deciduous trees up towards Erchless Castle. The route continues to follow the river passing through beautiful scenery back towards the village of Beauly.

*From single track to swooping wide roads, this route has some spectacular sections of road.*

# 54 APPLECROSS: A COASTAL CRUISE

**Start point:** Strathcarron railway station

**Grid ref:** NG 94217 42106

**Postcode:** IV54 8YR

**Total distance:** 102km

**Total elevation:** 2054m

**Max elevation:** 624m

## KEY CLIMBS

**From km 4 to km 9:** 140m climb over 5km

**From km 16.5 to km 26:** 614m climb over 9.5km

**From km 62 to km 65:** 122m climb over 3km

**From km 73 to km 80:** 120m climb over 7km

**From km 84.5 to km 93.5:** 132m climb over 9km

**Exposure:** 4.5/5

This Highland classic takes you up through Coire na Bà and Bealach na Bà before descending down to the small fishing port of Applecross. From this tranquil little village, head north along the coast with the inner sound out to your left and spectacular views over to the Isle of Skye. Clinging to the coastline, head up to Loch Torridon before heading inland through the Glen Shieldaig Forest. This truly spectacular route takes in some superb roads with a tough but rewarding climb over Bealach na Bà. The narrow roads keep you busy as you switch left and right, dipping up and down through picturesque woodland and quaint seaside villages.

*Spectacular scenery on the West Coast, a road-ride paradise.*

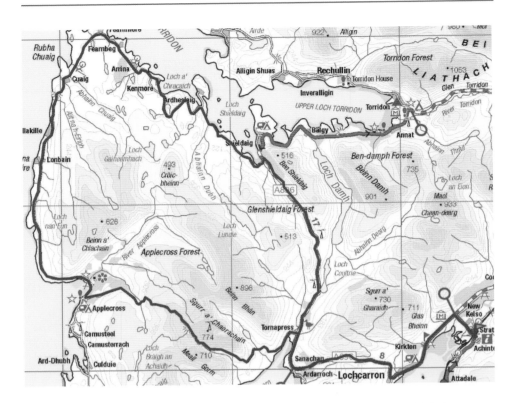

Applecross village.

From the railway station, pick up the A896 and follow the loch shore around to Lochcarron. The road climbs up through the stunning landscape and over to Loch Kishorn where you will start the climb up Bealach na Bà. This is a relatively tough

Let that be a warning to you!

climb and a series of steep switchbacks will lead you up on to the hilltops where there are some stunning views across to the Isle of Skye.

*The long descent down to Applecross.*

A long descent winds its way down to the sea and the fishing village of Applecross. The roads in this region are very narrow and can become busy throughout the summer holidays. Visibility is generally pretty good but do take care when passing oncoming traffic.

This route follows the coastline passing around Applecross Bay and on to the cliff tops above Inner Sound. Following the road northwards you get views out across Inner Sound to the Isle of Rassay and Isle of Skye. Continue northwards, hugging the coastline to the shores of Loch Torridon.

*The tough climb up Bealach na Bà is a really fantastic piece of road and quite unique in the UK.*

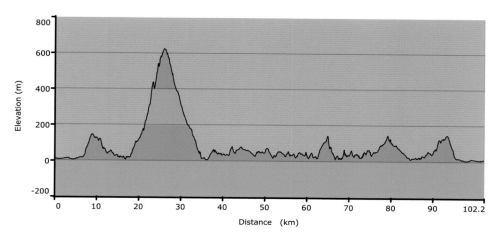

*Every corner opens up a new view and perspective on this stunning landscape.*

Here you have spectacular views with the mighty Beinn Alligin in the distance.

The road snakes its way along through breathtaking scenery as you head past Loch Shieldaig to the village of Shieldaig. A steep set of switchbacks bring you up to a T-junction where you take a right turn running along Glen Shieldaig on the A896. The road swings around the towering peaks and brings you back to Ardarroch village, here you retrace your steps back to the railway station at Strathcarron.

# 55 ACHNASHEEN: THE TORRIDON TERROR

**Start point:** Achnasheen railway station

**Grid ref:** NH 16359 58719

**Postcode:** IV22 2EJ

**Total distance:** 103km

**Total elevation:** 1430m

**Max elevation:** 253m

## KEY CLIMBS

**From km 16 to km 21.5:** 96m climb over 5.5km

**From km 33.5 to km 36.5:** 110m climb over 3km

**From km 41.5 to km 50.5:** 126m climb over 9km

**From km 56 to km 65:** 135m climb over 9km

**From km 69.5 to km 89.5:** 195m climb over 10km

**Exposure:** 4.5/5

This superb Highland route takes you up through Glentoran and covers just over 100 kilometres and near on 1500 metres of climbing. There are some spectacular views as you pass through many Munros, lochs and forests. The stunning Highland scenery continues to unfold as you head around Ben Shieldaig through Glen Shieldaig Forest down to Ardarroch village at the tip of Loch Kishorn. The route then makes its way up past Loch Carron, climbing up through Achnashellach Forest and Glen Carron back to the remote station at Achnasheen.

*The road to Torridon, spectacular.*

*Amazing views as you head out from the station.*

*The road may be tough but the scenery just keeps giving and giving.*

From the station, take a right turn at the roundabout on to the A832. Within a kilometre, join the northern shores of Loch a' Chroisg. The steep-sided hillside of An Liathach looms over you to the south as you head west along the loch side. At the end of the loch the road climbs up through woodland over a small pass before descending down through a steep-sided and truly stunning valley along Glen Docherty.

In the small village of Kinlochewe, take a left turn on to the Wester Ross Coastal Trail. This single-track road runs below the towering peaks of Beinn Eighe and Liathach that form part of Torridon Forest. This truly amazing section of road along Glen Torridon is something you need to see and ride.

You will then climb up above the southern shore of Upper Loch Torridon and on

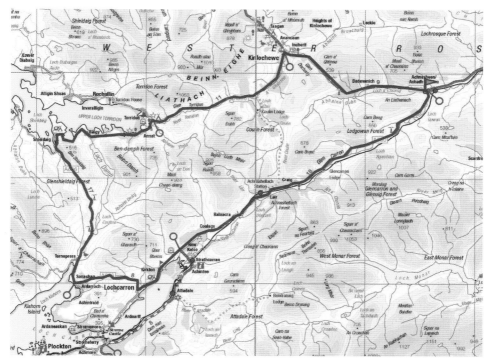

*This is a truly stunning part of the British Isles.*

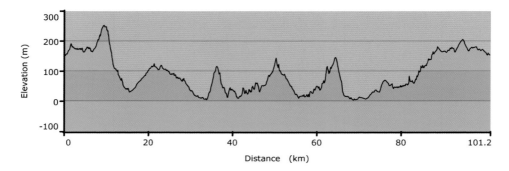

to Shieldaig village. The road climbs up Glen Shieldaig before descending down to Ardarroch village. If you wanted to make a real monster ride then just before the village you can take a right turn up on to the Applecross route on pages 200–201.

The route continues to follow the A896 heading east through Lochcarron before joining the A890 back towards Achnasheen. Climbing up, join the railway lines that pass through Achnashellach Station. As you ride, you will be clinging to the hillside and dipping in and out of the forests. Further up through Glen Carron the road becomes very exposed and there is little shelter should you encounter those easterly winds. The road continues to climb back up to the roundabout at Achnasheen where you started the route.

*Lochs, glens and fast descents.*

# APPENDIX: GIRO D'ITALIA 2014, GRANDE PARTENZA ON THE EMERALD ISLE

For the keen racing fans out there you can follow in the wheels of the world's elite over in Ireland as the opening stages of the 2014 Giro d'Italia start in Belfast. Three days of great racing will take the riders through some superb scenery. A time trial kicks off the proceedings before they head out of Belfast from the Antrim Road on a 218km stage around the north-east coastline of county Antrim. The route takes the riders through Antrim, Ballymena and Bushmills, passing the Giant's Causeway, hugging the coastline from Cushendall to Larne then onto Whitehead and Carrickfergus, before dropping back into Belfast.

The third and final stage in Ireland links from Armagh down the east coast through Castlebellingham and Balbriggan before entering Dublin, another long day in the saddle for the riders as they cover 187km. From Armagh the route passes through Richhill and onto Newtonhamilton, heading south over the border at Forkhill and on towards Dublin, passing through Dundalk, Castlebellingham and Drogheda.

The routes take in some quieter back roads but being a pro tour there are a lot of main roads used in the routes. Of course, you could avoid the latter and easily make up a ride that takes in the more interesting quieter roads used in the Giro while exploring Ireland.

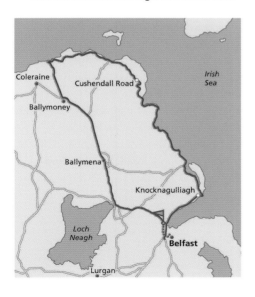

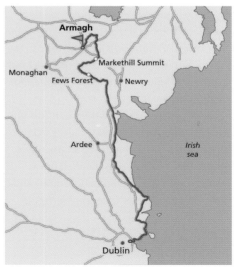

# ACKNOWLEDGEMENTS

This is the hardest part for me when it comes to writing a book. I'm sorry if I missed anyone one but I'm very fortunate (and thankful) to know so many loving cool cats. As I could ramble for ages with shout outs to many people who have helped and inspired me over the years, I'll try to keep it brief.

Daria, my dearest wife and inspiration, thank you for your love, support and guidance with this book. I'm for ever your guy. I'd like to thank and bless my late parents Vickie and Bob, without their love and support I'd never have made my childhood dreams come true. I'd also like to thank my brother Kevin, the strongest, most kind-hearted person. Love you, bro.

Big thanks to David from MyOsteo, Wendy and family. Cheers for keeping my body capable, Dave – you're the best bone-cruncher in the South!

A massive thank you and big love to my Tuscan family, Piera, Maurizio, Giorgia (and family) and Valerio. Thank you so much for welcoming me into your world.

To all my sponsors for their continued support. Special mention to Jamie from Boardman Bikes – cheers for an awesome ride, truly amazing bike. Mitchell from Mavic, cheers for the fantastic wheels and fine clothing – they made the journey a swift and luxurious experience. Simon from Garmin, many thanks for the great Edge 800 unit and mapping software, a real asset to the project and a superb unit to work with. Cheers to Jimmy and the team at Mule Bar for fuelling my adventures. Thanks to Matt at Chaineys Cycles, John and the team at The Cycle Centre, Mark at Next Level, Steve Dees at I-Cycles and the team at Future Publishing and Factory Media.

Big thanks to my riding buddies of many years: Gavin, Pip, Barry, Jonathan, Mark, Guy, Steve, Tally, Wendy, Jam Master J, Andy 'Wednesday' Marshall, Ian Marshall (and Mrs Marshall), Robbie Richmond and family, Rachel, Big Mark, Potsy, Jemma and all the gang in D&G. Massive thanks to Chris Walker and all of you in the south.

Frazer, keep the faith, bro. You're a hugely talented individual and I'm forever grateful for your amazing images and friendship. You know you've been on the road too long when...

Many thanks to Charlotte and the team at Bloomsbury for all your hard work.

Finally to those we have lost and dearly miss: John Flood, Adam Jakeman and Vanessa Atkins. All of you are forever in our minds and hearts.

# INDEX